NEW YORK
OPEN TO THE PUBLIC

The Garibaldi-Meucci Museum

Bronx Zoo

Staten Island Children's Museum

The Interchurch Center

Museum of the American Indian

The New York Botanical Garden

Jacques Marchais Center

Schomburg Center

Queens Botanical Garden Society

The Staten Island Zoo

Cooper-Hewitt

Marine Museum

Japan House Gallery

The Fulton Ferry Museum

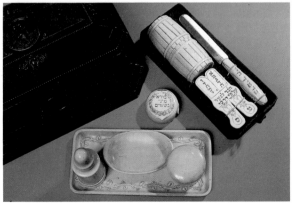

Ferkauf Museum

Chinese Museum

Overleaf:
Thè Panorama of New York City at the Queens Museum.

NEW Y

OPEN TO

A Comprehensive Guide to

STEWART, TABORI & CHANG

CHERI FEIN

PHOTOGRAPHS BY

Joseph Kugielski

ORK
THE PUBLIC

*Museums, Collections,
Exhibition Spaces, Historic Houses,
Botanical Gardens and Zoos*

PUBLISHERS, NEW YORK

EDITED BY: Marya Dalrymple

DESIGNED BY: Nai Chang

Library of Congress Cataloging in Publication Data

Fein, Cheri.
  New York—open to the public.

  Includes index.
    1. New York (N.Y.)—Description—1981—Guide-
books. 2. Museums—New York (N.Y.)—Guide-
books. 3. Botanical gardens—New York (N.Y.)—
Guide-books. 4. Exhibition buildings—New York
(N.Y.)—Guide-books. 5. Historic buildings—New
York (N.Y.)—Guide-books. 6. Zoological
gardens—New York (N.Y.)—Guide-books.
I. Kugielsky, Joseph. II. Title.
F128.18.F38   917.47'10443   81-21468
ISBN 0-941434-00-1   AACR2

Text ©1982 by Cheri Fein

Photographs ©1982 by Joseph Kugielsky

Distributed by Workman Publishing Company,
Inc., 1 West 39th Street, New York, New York
10018

Printed in Italy

for George

—C. F.

for Lila and Anne

—J. K.

Table of Contents

Introduction

The lyricist Betty Comden was right. New York *is* a wonderful town. Not that I wasn't already convinced of it. But researching and writing *New York: Open to the Public* has given me the luxury of a focused, in-depth view afforded few New Yorkers. It has been an extraordinary and humbling experience.

After living in New York for more than a decade, I figured I'd been around—culturally, that is. How many out-of-the-way museums, unusual collections, or hidden treasures could anyone point out that I hadn't at least heard of? As it turned out, plenty. Visiting over 150 museums, collections, exhibition and alternative art spaces, historic houses, botanical gardens, and zoos substantially altered my perspective. It showed me just what I had been missing.

I discovered the treasures at the Songwriters Hall of Fame Museum and at Aunt Len's Doll and Toy Museum. I learned that the Brooklyn Children's Museum, a high-tech extravaganza, is the oldest children's museum in the world. I found that in every borough, nestled in pocket parks or crammed between highrises and parking lots, are gambrel-roofed farmhouses and fine old mansions that survived the Revolutionary War.

I realized that New York's museums and exhibition spaces are everywhere—in a clock-tower, on a barge on the Hudson River, in a subway station, on the site of a former rest home for sailors, in old schoolhouses and townhouses. They are built on grounds that have been an ash dump, a reservoir, even a potter's field. Wherever there is available space, it seems that someone has stepped in to transform it into a place that will give people pleasure. But with so much to choose from, where do you start?

Figuring it made some sense to begin not only near the city's southernmost tip, where the first settlers lived, but also at a spot notable in American history, I started at Fraunces Tavern Museum in lower Manhattan. It was here, in the Long Room of the tavern, that George Washing-ton bid an emotional farewell to his officers on December 4, 1783, before leaving for Annapolis to resign his commission. Washington would return soon enough to New York, this time for an even more important ceremony—his inauguration as the first President of the United States, an event that took place at my second stop, Federal Hall. Ultimately, my visits didn't follow such an historical or logical plan. I skipped around from borough to borough, mixing the big museums with the small ones, visiting an art space and then a zoo, fully enjoying and taking advantage of the city's amazing diversity.

The major museums alone were enough to fill a book. I spent an entire day at the Met, wandering through the American Wing and the Astor Court, marveling that it is possible to house entire temples and gardens under a single roof. But the Met is like that, always sprouting new wings like some mythic beast, always changing, while never depriving you of its permanent collections. The American Museum of Natural History, the Guggenheim, the Whitney, and the city's other greats are the same, changing but dependable. Take the Museum of Modern Art, which is currently building an elaborate high-rise extension onto the old building. It's still the place I run to when I'm in a gray mood, for I know that the Matisses and Gauguins will always be there to cheer me up.

It was the small places, however, that most genuinely intrigued me. Some were astonishingly quirky, all were absolutely fascinating. In fact, the first entry in *New York: Open to the Public* is a place I had never visited but now plan to regularly. ABC No Rio isn't well known, but more is happening in this single, falling-down room on Manhattan's Lower East Side than in many of the city's more publicized exhibition spaces. I felt the energy as soon as I walked in. Art was being made here, raw and risky. I had never seen anything like it before.

Another of the book's finds is a townhouse just off the Bowery, which I had walked by any number of times. The house is the last elegant holdout on a street that has seen better days. I often wondered who lived there, who had lived there in the past, and just how the house had managed to survive. More than once I had paused at the gate, straining to get a glimpse through the windows. Imagine my surprise and delight when I learned that the house was a museum. All one had to do to visit was to come by on any Sunday afternoon. I did, and stepping through the door of the Old Merchant's House was like stepping into a time capsule. Every detail was so meticulously preserved that I actually felt like a trespasser, not only into a private home, but into the nineteenth century.

Many times I found that the exterior of a place gave no clue to the collection inside. Aunt Len's is like that. One day, having arranged an appointment, I stood on the stoop of her house on pretty Hamilton Terrace in upper Manhattan and rang the doorbell. Aunt Len herself directed me through a narrow hallway cluttered with tables and vases and pictures. When we descended a steep flight of steps to her basement, I discovered what surely no other person keeps in such an unlikely spot: dolls, over 3,000 of them, dressed in every possible costume, from Betty Boop to Howdy Doody, their faces radiating every possible expression.

I was just as surprised at the Songwriters Hall of Fame, which is hidden away on the eighth floor of a Times Square building. You don't have to get past the Tin Pan Alley piano standing near the door to realize that the people who work here love both music and the place. Music is their world, and best of all they want to share it. "Touch these instruments," they say. "Play them. Look at this old sheet music. Remember that tune?"

It was on an early summer morning that I walked onto the boardwalk at Coney Island, looked across a still-uncluttered stretch of beach to the Atlantic Ocean, and found it hard to accept the fact that I was still in New York City. This was not the Coney Island of collapsing roller coasters and Nathan's Famous Hotdogs, but a seaside place where the ocean misted your face at about the same rate as the sun dried it. As I settled down on a bench across from the sign that read "New York Aquarium" and looked out at the ocean, all I could think was how perfect it is that the aquarium is located here and not in the middle of Times Square. Going out to Coney Island from Manhattan was a

real change of pace—a mini-vacation. But so was visiting the Cloisters, the Frick Collection, the Brooklyn Botanic Garden, and Snug Harbor. I had forgotten that this crash-bang metropolis has refuges that are tranquil, that smell good, that refresh the spirit. I had forgotten how very easy it is to escape the hubbub by simply walking through a door or a gate.

With the current funding cutbacks, however, it seems inevitable that more than a few of these doors will close. Even now, from the mega-museums to the modest, the strain can be felt. When I stop to think about the difficulties of funding, I realize how incredible it is that the places in this book exist at all. How does a museum begin? And how does it manage to survive? I kept asking these questions and getting the same answer: It is people who keep these worlds turning, people with the kind of passion and tenacity that transcends the problems of how to continue. They are the neighbors who banded together to create El Museo del Barrio so that their children would know their heritage; the collectors, like Aunt Len, who are generous enough to share what they have gathered; the people in a community who refuse to watch an important historic house, such as the Old Merchant's, deteriorate or be torn down; the young ABC No Rio artists who push exhibition spaces beyond the predictable and established so that art remains an innovative and vital force in the world. Meeting these people and seeing what they have built and maintained has perhaps been an even more fascinating experience for me than visiting the places themselves.

If during these months there was a single time when many different feelings surfaced at once, it was the shimmery August day when I took the ferry to the Museum of Immigration at the Statue of Liberty. As the boat pulled close to Our Lady and she loomed taller and more dignified than ever, I was overwhelmed with the realization of how fortunate I am to have so many pleasures available to me in this city. I turned toward the Manhattan skyline; I looked over at Staten Island's hills and the coastline of Brooklyn; I thought about Queens and the Bronx, now familiar to me, and about all of the extraordinary places I had visited in each of these boroughs. As I scanned this horizon I was suddenly filled with a tremendous burst of energy and a desire to keep on exploring. *New York: Open to the Public*, I realized, was just a beginning.

Acknowledgments

Many thanks to the following friends and colleagues whose help was invaluable to me in writing this book: Daniel Morper, Jerry Chasen, Charlotte Sheedy, Jana Harris, Bill Rayman, Eric Rayman, Marya Dalrymple, Beth Harnick, Marsha Melnick, Susan Meyer, and Christian Czyz. I am most grateful to all of the curators and administrators at the museums, exhibition spaces, historic houses, botanical gardens, and zoos who gave so much of their time and energy. Without them this book would not have been possible.—C.F.

I would like to thank Michael Petraglia for his unfaltering assistance and some valuable lessons, and Anne Kugielsky for a seven-day work week.—J.K.

How to Use This Book

I chose the places in *New York: Open to the Public* because they *are* open for public viewing and because their collections or exhibits are of lasting or special interest. It was not an easy task to limit my selection. Certainly Radio City Music Hall, the Empire State Building, Rockefeller Center, the New York Stock Exchange, and many of the city's commercial art galleries are some of New York's most popular attractions, but these and other places like them did not readily fit my criteria for this book and are therefore not listed.

The book is organized alphabetically for easy reference, with each entry appearing under its proper name: the Guggenheim can be found as the Solomon R. Guggenheim Museum, and Richmondtown Restoration is listed as part of the Staten Island Historical Society, for example. Two indexes present the entries by the borough in which they are located and by category. Each place has also been pinpointed on one of the five borough maps provided.

Complete addresses and telephone numbers have been given for each entry, and the nearest cross streets and main thoroughfares are indicated in parentheses to enable easy access. It is advisable to telephone before visiting a place to make certain that it is open and, for the smaller places, that there is an exhibition mounted. Some of the smaller museums or collections may require an advance appointment; don't be discouraged, the appointments are not difficult to schedule.

You will note that each of the main entries in the book also provides information on hours, admission fees, services, and access by subway, bus, and car. For the subway, I have listed the train numbers or letters and the nearest stops. Bus numbers have been provided for Manhattan and parts of Staten Island only; if you wish to find out which Manhattan buses run to the boroughs, call the Metropolitan Transit Authority Travel Information Service at (212) 330-1234. The MTA also runs two "culture buses," which stop near many of the museums. Bus maps are available at the Pennsylvania Station MTA office. For those who choose to drive, parking information is supplied, and directions have been given for driving from Manhattan to each of the museums in the boroughs (please note that I have indicated only *one* way to get to each place; there are others).

The symbols (see symbol code below) provided for each entry will let you know at a glance if food and gifts are available, whether wheelchairs, strollers, children (with parents), and photography are allowed, and whether lectures and tours are given. An "X" through a symbol indicates that a particular service is *not* available.

Food   Wheelchairs   Strollers   Children   Lectures   Tours   Photographs   Research   Gifts

The building is almost collapsing. The space itself is a crazy quilt of colors splattered on the walls, low-hanging pipes, a decrepit refrigerator in the corner, and an uneven floor with a hole in it. It is a storefront, flanked on either side by hangouts for drug addicts, which has been converted into the semblance of a gallery. It is ABC No Rio, and it is presenting the truest and most exciting issue-oriented exhibits in the city.

The whole thing started in January 1980 with an event called the *Real Estate Show*, in which artists took over an abandoned building on Delancey Street and mounted an exhibition. The city came in and closed the place, but some of the artists pressed on and found the Rivington Street location and City Hall said okay.

The artists certainly didn't expect to stay set up for any length of time, but four of them did remain and now run ABC No Rio with an easygoing wit and no salary. (The name came from a notary public's faded sign written in Spanish.)

But a haphazard air belies an intent that is really quite serious. This is apparent by the type of shows that are put together—all solidly political, although the gallery claims no political affiliation.

The inaugural exhibition, called *Artists for Survival*, had an antinuclear theme. Two of the pieces in that show were a lead raincoat and a sculpture garden that included life-sized cement rats burrowing through rubble.

Artists for Survival was followed by *Suicide, Murder and Junk*, which was organized by a heroin addict with some work done by neighborhood people and junkies. In the next show the walls were plastered with political posters internationally solicited by the San Francisco Poster Brigade. Sometime later, *City Wildlife* went up; it addressed the issue of vermin in the urban landscape and people's reactions to its presence. Household pets were displayed alongside wild infesters such as pigeons, roaches, and rats. The health department was brought in for workshops on preventing infestation, and a roach behaviorist from the American Museum of Natural History gave a lecture.

The exhibition schedule follows no orderly pattern, but the space is generally open for anyone who wants to come by to make art (some materials are provided) and to attend the frequent performances, readings, and meetings.

Hours: M: 7 P.M.-8 P.M., W-Sa: 2-7. Closed major holidays.
Admission free.
Picture-taking by permission.
Access: Subway: F to Delancey Street; J, M to Essex Street. Bus: M15. Car: Metered street parking and garage parking nearby.

17

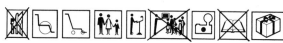

Abigail Adams Smith Museum

421 East 61st Street, New York, N.Y. 10021 (212) 838-6878

At one time this sturdy stone building rested on 23 acres of land owned by William Stephen Smith and his wife, Abigail Adams Smith, the daughter of John Adams. The structure was built as a carriage house, intended to complement the Smiths' home, Mount Vernon. The East River, just 50 feet from the door, offered a fine view and turtles for making green turtle soup. The city was five miles south, and the year was 1795.

It is extraordinary that the building has survived, that this bit of land has not been leveled but remains a high hill, shielded from Sixty-first Street traffic by a stone wall and hedges. But there it is, at the foot of the Queensboro Bridge, a lovely H-shaped house on a half acre of tidy ground.

The Smiths were forced to sell their land before the dream mansion was finished, and the carriage house, completed in 1799, underwent some changes. In the 1820s it was the Mount Vernon Hotel, later a private house, and in the early 1900s it served as an office building. Finally, in 1924, it was purchased by the Colonial Dames of America, who opened the museum in 1939, in time for the New York World's Fair.

At the front door, you can use either a shiny brass knocker or a door pull that tinkles an unseen bell. Inside are nine rooms furnished predominantly in the Federal style (dating from 1790 to 1820). In the dining room you will find American Sheraton chairs that belonged to Abigail Adams Smith. The music room has a harp, piano, and barrel organ. In the kitchen, near the open hearth, are two tin reflector ovens and a brass bed warmer.

A wide stairway with a polished hardwood banister, probably from the days when the building served as an inn, leads from the first floor to the second. There you will find a wooden cradle; handmade toys; a dress made and worn by Abigail Adams Smith; whale oil lamps; John Adams's Presidential Seal; letters from Adams, James Monroe, and George Washington; and more lovely furniture. Each room is quite complete, from wallpaper and rugs to candlesticks and birdcages. And although Abigail Adams Smith never had the chance to keep her carriage here, her name has remained associated with a most attractive and interesting place.

Hours: M-F: 10-4. Closed August and major holidays.

Admission fee charged. Children under twelve free.

Research facilities available to scholars by appointment.

Access: Subway: #4, 5, 6 to 59th Street; N, RR to Lexington Avenue. Bus: M15, 31, 103. Car: Parking nearby.

19

The African-American Institute

833 United Nations Plaza (47th Street and First Avenue), New York, N.Y. 10017 (212) 949-5666

The bright costumes, wooden sculptures, or fine batiks exhibited behind the large plate-glass windows of the African-American Institute are as effective an attraction as a department store's window displays. Located across from the United Nations, this attractive storefront is the African-American Institute's lobby.

The AAI is the major private organization in the United States working to further African development, inform Americans about Africa, and strengthen African-American understanding. It concerns itself with human development and racial equality. It also organizes travel in Africa, provides services to American corporations and banks that have interests there, and aids individuals who want to do research, study, or work in Africa.

The institute's exhibition space is of modest size—just the lobby and a small gallery which is reached by passing through an office area. But the African art and artists who are featured in the three annual exhibitions are of the highest caliber. For example, the 1979 exhibition of 115 traditional sculptures from Upper Volta was the first major exhibit of Voltaic art to be held in New York since a 1972 exhibit at the now-defunct Museum of Primitive Art.

The exhibitions of traditional and contemporary arts and crafts, organized thematically and in solo or small group shows, are drawn from museums and private collections. Coming to us from such a large and diverse continent, the work is always interesting.

If what you see in the lobby window are fantastic costumes with bright embroidery and appliqués, be assured that in the gallery you will find other equally wonderful pieces—perhaps the costumes used for ritual masquerades in the northern Edo region of Nigeria. If what catches your glance is a wooden goat that doubles as a cage, it could be a piece from a show on art for and by African children. Whether it be ancient terra cottas from Ghana and Mali or leather masks from Zaire embedded with shells, beads, and metal, the African-American Institute assembles fascinating exhibitions that instruct and always give pleasure.

Hours: M-F: 9-5, Sa: 11-5. Closed major holidays. Admission free.
Tours in English and French by appointment.
  Picture-taking by permission. Research
  facilities available by appointment.
Access: Subway: #4, 5, 6, 7 to 42nd Street.
  Bus: M27, 104. Car: Parking nearby.

20

Alternative Museum

17 White Street (Sixth Avenue), New York, N.Y. 10013   (212) 966-4444

The Alternative Museum is a place to visit if you want a preview of what might be appearing in American museums in the coming years. Founded by artists, this white-pillared, 3,000-square-foot, ground floor loft aims to give non-mainstream, nonestablished painters and sculptors an opportunity to show their work.

The exhibits found here frequently carry such up-to-the-minute titles as *Post Modernist Metaphors, New Imagists, Emerging Artists,* and *Young Contemporaries,* and the paintings and sculptures often have sci-fi- or media- influenced names like *Biochemical Vignette, The Blue Novena Fighters of the Darkness, Ring IV,* and *Jaws II.* Whether figurative or abstract, the works have been pushed to the limits of acceptability—in image, color, line, or materials. Still, the quality of the art is uncompromising, and the exhibits, which change 12 to 15 times a year and are guest curated by critics, scholars, and artists, are of high professional standards. A small area at the entrance is reserved for work from the museum's permanent collection.

A separate but important aspect of the Alternative Museum is its World Music Series, which is committed to the concept that all music influences other music to create "One World." The Saturday evening series presents live concerts performed by an international lineup of musicians.

Hours: W-Sa: 11-6. Closed July, August, and Christmas through New Year's Day.
Admission free.
Access: Subway: #1 to Franklin Street; A, AA, CC, E to Canal Street. Bus: M6, 10. Car: Parking lot nearby.

American Bible Society

1865 Broadway (61st Street), New York, N.Y. 10023   (212) 581-7400

The *Good News Bible* is displayed in one window of the American Bible Society. In another window is *Dios habla hoy*—the *Good News* translated into Spanish. And once again, in the third window is the *Good News Bible*, this time in Chinese. Since its founding in 1816, the American Bible Society has had one purpose: "To promote the distribution of Holy Scriptures. . . ."

Once inside you walk up the white circular stairs covered with tomato red carpeting. Here is the library of 39,000 volumes—a collection of Bibles and books on the Bible written in nearly 1,600 languages. To the left, dramatically presented in a glass room set high above the main room, are rare Bibles dating from 1275 to 1700. To the right are exhibition cases for permanent and temporary displays: a replica of the Gutenberg Press is the centerpiece for a permanent exhibit on the Gutenberg Bible. Here are facsimile pages, a map of the Bibles' locations, and information on Johannes Gutenberg, who was the inventor of movable type and the special ink required for printing.

The Dead Sea Scrolls constitute another permanent exhibit—a display of fragments from the scrolls' sheepskin parchment and wrapping and a replica of one of the urns that contained the scrolls when they were discovered in 1947

by shepherds near the Dead Sea.

Also on permanent display is Helen Keller's Bible, including all twelve volumes printed in braille.

Temporary exhibits (changing every four to six months) include such themes as miniature Bibles, which became quite fashionable when first produced in 1614; polyglot Bibles containing versions of the same text in different languages (such as a 1591 Gospels in Latin and Arabic); and Bible woodcuts, including the 1550 Danish interpretation of the Lost Ark as a little cart with wheels.

Upon request, a librarian will take you into a back room to see an extraordinary item in the collection: a torah written in Hebrew from the Chinese province of Honan, where a community of Chinese Jews lived from the thirteenth to the fifteenth century.

Hours: M-F: 9:30-4:30. Closed major holidays. Admission free.

Lectures and tours in English, Spanish, Chinese, Hungarian, German, French, Greek, and Finnish by appointment. Picture-taking by permission. Research facilities available to scholars only.

Access: Subway: A, AA, CC, D to 59th Street. Bus: M5, 7, 104. Car: Garage parking nearby.

22

American Craft Museum

44 West 53rd Street, New York, N.Y. 10019 (212) 397-0630

At the American Craft Museum art is vases and pitchers and pots, dresses and vests and plates, spoons and violins and boxes—all handcrafted with the greatest concern for quality and design by contemporary masters. Here are objects you want to run your hands over, care for, own—a glass pitcher to fill with iced tea, an inlaid ebony box for secreting valuables, sterling silver flatware so graceful you wouldn't even mind polishing it.

The atmosphere at the American Craft Museum is quite intimate. The works on display bear the personal marks of the talented craftspeople who made them. In the case of a clay mug, the handle has been molded in the shape of the craftsperson's grip. If you owned that mug, every time you picked it up to take a sip of coffee you would in essence grasp the artist's hand. The tactile nature of the crafts poses one of the museum's biggest problems: Many visitors have great difficulty abiding by the Do Not Touch rule.

Founded in 1956 and administered by the American Craft Council, a national membership organization, the American Craft Museum was the first museum in the country devoted entirely to crafts. It has always been interested in documenting excellence, reviving old techniques, and exploring new methods.

The three major exhibitions mounted each year are organized thematically and cover a wide range of craft techniques. *The Clay Figure*, *For the Tabletop* (glassware, dinnerware, and cutlery), *New Handmade Furniture*, *The Harmonious Craft* (musical instruments), and *The Great American Foot* (a tribute to guess what) have been a few of the recent presentations. Often demonstrations and workshops accompany the exhibits. In the case of *The Harmonious Craft*, for example, there was a workshop on how to make instruments from objects found in the home.

The museum itself is not large, yet the space is open and inviting and the wonderful pieces are well displayed. In fact, partly because of the need for more exhibition space, the museum is undergoing an expansion that will turn the Fifty-third Street space into number one of two. In May 1982, American Craft Museum II, sponsored by International Paper and located in that company's new world headquarters, is opening eight blocks to the south. Designed by the Space Design Group, the large ground-floor gallery sits adjacent to the plaza that runs between Forty-fifth and Forty-sixth Streets.

Hours: Tu-Sa: 10-5, Su: 11-5. Closed major holidays and between exhibitions.
Admission fee charged.
Picture-taking by permission. Research facilities available by appointment.
Access: Subway: E, F to Fifth Avenue. Bus: M1, 2, 3, 4, 5, 6, 7, 32. Car: Parking lots nearby.

American Craft Museum II, International Paper Plaza, 77 West 45th Street, New York, N.Y. 10036. Opens May, 1982.

23

The American Museum of Immigration

Statue of Liberty National Monument, Liberty Island, New York, N.Y. 10004   (212) 732-1236

For the 12 million excited and exhausted immigrants who landed at Ellis Island between 1892 and 1954, the graceful copper lady lifting her lamp on nearby Liberty Island was the first reassuring indication that the golden door of America would indeed open to them.

Even today for those of us who were born in this country, the Statue of Liberty, appearing from a distance to rise right out of the waters of New York Harbor, is a thrilling sight.

Her formal name is "Statue of Liberty Enlightening the World." She was given to the United States by France in recognition of ties first formed during the American Revolution and unveiled on October 28, 1886. Her height is 151 feet; the pedestal is an additional 154 feet.

The pedestal rests within the star-shaped walls of the former Fort Wood, built in the first half of the nineteenth century as a part of New York's harbor defense. Here, at this base, is the American Museum of Immigration, whose exhibit tells in chronological order the stories of the 40 nationalities that have melted into this pot called the United States.

Starting with the sixteenth-century Spanish settlements in Puerto Rico, Florida, and Texas, the rather dizzying tour covers such diverse cultures as the English, Dutch, French, Polish, Irish, Latvian, Ukrainian, Russian, Italian, and Chinese, all people who left their homelands for various reasons: to escape war, famine, and persecution; for economic opportunities and political freedom; for the pure adventure of making it in the land that had "streets paved with gold."

What these people brought with them—lace, samovars, Belleek china, candlesticks—and how they used their talents once here—Duncan Phyfe furniture, crystal, art—are on display. You will see reproductions of 1850s clothing showing what your great-grandparents might have worn off the boat and a wall-sized photograph of a Lower East Side street telling the real-life story of the huddled masses.

Two of the most compelling objects are artifacts of persecution. The first is a terrifying iron manacle from a slave ship. (Slaves were the one exception to the reasons given for immigration; theirs was forced.) The second is a Torah that was smuggled into a concentration camp at Vittel, France, and was used at the first Jewish services at Dachau and Mauthausen in 1945.

The statue and museum are easily reached by a ferry that leaves from Battery Park. You will find that the ferry ride is a decidedly more sanguine journey than that of our ancestors.

Hours: Daily: 9:15-5. June through September: 9-6:15. Closed Christmas.
Admission free.
Tours in many languages upon request.
Access: Subway to Liberty Island Ferry: #1 to South Ferry; #4, 5 to Bowling Green; N, RR to Whitehall Street. Bus to Liberty Island Ferry: M1, 6. Car: Parking at Ferry limited weekdays.

24

Photographs except Hayden Planetarium by Jonathan Wallen

The American Museum of Natural History prefers to do things in a big way. Its idea of wildlife is a herd of East African elephants charging toward you from the center of a room. Its idea of a mammal is a 94-foot model of a female blue whale, suspended in midair as if she were taking a dive through the waves. Its idea of a minerals and gems exhibit is one that displays 6,000 specimens. Its idea of subject matter is the universe.

You would need roller skates and a degree in speed-reading to cover this museum in a single visit. (The collections include about 34 million artifacts and specimens!) Better to pick out a few favorite areas and concentrate on these.

People watchers might begin with the biology of man exhibit and move on to the displays of various cultures—American Indian, African, and Asian peoples. The extraordinary, lifelike scenes displayed in the many dioramas are quite moving. More dioramas will be featured in the Margaret Mead Hall of Pacific Peoples, which will be open in early 1983. The hall is named for the eminent anthropologist who made the Natural History Museum her professional home for 52 years.

Monster-movie fans who want to get the real facts about the subject should visit the dinosaurs on display—prehistoric animals that are sufficiently numerous to warrant being divided into early- and late-period rooms. (The museum is probably best known for these skeletons of earth's previous tenants.) Other earth creatures you may want to visit include mammal and bird specimens from all parts of the world, 230,000 reptiles and amphibians, and more than 15 million insects.

Two of the most fascinating exhibits are the Arthur Ross Halls of Meteorites and the Hall of Minerals and Gems. The focal point of the Arthur Ross Halls is Ahnighito ("The Tent"), a meteorite that fell on Cape York, Greenland,

---

Hours: M, Tu, W, F: 10-4:45, W: 10-8, Sa & Su: 10-5.

Admission by donation.

Tours in English, French, Spanish, Japanese, Italian, Chinese, and Russian by advance appointment. Picture-taking without tripod permitted.

Access: Subway: AA, CC to 81st Street. Bus: M10, 17. Car: Parking lot on premises.

about 10,000 years ago; it is the largest ever extracted from the earth's surface. The minerals and gems have mysterious names like cryolite, almandine, chalcanthite. Shining and stunning, they are arranged in demystifying displays that explain their properties, their environments, their interaction with energy, and their aesthetics. The most coveted rock in this collection is the Star of India sapphire. Mined in Ceylon three centuries ago and presented to the museum by J. P. Morgan, it weighs 563.35 carats and is nearly free from flaws.

After seeing such earth wonders, you may choose to visit the Hayden Planetarium. There you can learn what your weight would be on the sun, moon, and other planets (one bonus of go-

29

ing to the moon is that you would weigh one-sixth of your earth weight). Or you can travel through a mysterious blacklit hall containing large murals of the lunar landscape, solar eclipses, and spiral nebulas. But most compelling is the show in the main theater, where, under the dome of a perfectly clear, star-filled sky, you can rest and reflect on how such an amazing world came to be.

Hayden Planetarium

Hours: M-F: 12-4:45, Sa & Su: 10-6. July through September: M-F: 12-4:45, Sa & Su: 12-5.

Admission fee charged. Free if you enter from the American Museum of Natural History. No children under two allowed.

Access: Same as American Museum of Natural History.

The American Numismatic Society

Broadway at 155th Street, New York, N.Y. 10032   (212) 234-3130

Photographs courtesy of the American Numismatic Society

Hours: Tu-Sa: 9-4:30, Su: 1-3. Closed major
   holidays.
Admission free.
Wheelchairs accommodated by appointment.
   Occasional lectures. Tours by appointment.
Access: Subway: #1 to 157th Street; A, AA, B,
   CC, D to 155th Street. Bus: M4, 5. Car:
   Metered street parking nearby.

Although coins tend to be regarded as collectibles, they are actually crucial historical documents that tell stories of war, trade, politics, and culture. Coins can serve as items for political propaganda (i.e., whose image gets on a coin) and can function as message bearers (e.g., Islamic coins, which quote passages from the Koran).

The word *numismatic* means the study of coins and medals, particularly from an archaeological or historical standpoint, and that is exactly what the American Numismatic Society does—it collects and studies coins, as it has been doing since 1858.

Although the imposing Indiana limestone building on the south side of Audubon Terrace is primarily a research facility with an extremely fine library and a highly trained staff, you can ring the bell and a guard will let you in to see the two exhibition rooms.

The rooms, which are on either side of the entrance, have exhibits that in theory change. But because the staff is more interested in doing academic work than in performing curatorial duties, the displays have become more or less permanent.

In the East Gallery is a show called *Money In America,* which has been up since before the Bicentennial. There are coins from as early as 1652, when the first mint was set up in Boston, and there is paper money from 1776 in both shillings and dollars. Here you will also see Spanish dollars, which were a popular currency after the Revolution when money was available from Spanish possessions in Central and South America. Since the Spanish dollar was divided into eighths, the term *two bits* came to mean a quarter of a dollar, which is how "two bits, four bits, eight bits, a dollar" became a popular chant.

The West Gallery has cases of medals, medallions, and decorations covering such themes as animals, saints, composers, aviation, and transportation. In the center of the room are unusual ancient coins—pieces of eight that conjure up fantasies of pirates on the high seas and coins with Roman imperial portraits. To see the profiles of Nero, Tiberius, Hadrian, and Agrippina I (mother of Caligula) on objects that were actually in use during their lives is an absolutely thrilling experience.

32

TheAmerican-Scandinavian Foundation

127 East 73rd Street, New York, N.Y. 10021   (212) 879-9779

When an exhibition is up, a bright banner hangs from the flagpole at the American-Scandinavian Foundation's headquarters, a landmark townhouse once owned by the illustrator of hourglass-figured damsels Charles Dana Gibson.

Attached to Mr. Gibson's former residence, which was designed in 1903 by his friend Stanford White, is some classic historical gossip. Gibson was fond of using an artist's model who came to symbolize the Gibson girl. One unusual painting of her was in profile, with her long hair forming a question mark; he called this work "The Eternal Question." That model, Evelyn Nesbit, was the woman with whom Stanford White would fall in love and on whose account he would be killed by Harry K. Thaw in 1906.

On the second floor of the townhouse, in what was once the living quarters, are the rooms now used for exhibitions. In five to six shows a year, ASF presents the work of leading Scandinavian and Scandinavian-American artists. You might see the exquisite sculptural glass works of Norwegian artist Benny Motzfeldt, one of Europe's leading glass artists, or the stark beauty of Iceland as depicted in the prints of 17 graphic artists. Or the work of two Swedish silversmiths. Or colorfully patterned Finnish *rya* rugs.

ASF also co-sponsors more extensive shows, such as the mammoth Viking exhibition that was at the Metropolitan Museum of Art in late 1980; or the ambitious *Scandinavia Today* project, which from late 1982 through mid-1983 will bring exhibitions on painting, photography, design, textiles, and graphics to museums in major U.S. cities, including New York.

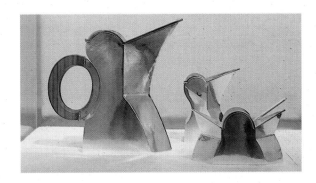

Hours: W-Sa: 12-5. Closed between exhibitions. Call before visiting.
Admission free.
Occasional lectures. Research facilities by advance appointment.
Access: Subway: #6 to 77th Street. Bus: M1, 2, 3, 4, 101, 102. Car: Garage parking nearby.

33

Americas Society—Center for Inter-American Relations

680 Park Avenue (68th Street), New York, N.Y. 10021   (212) 249-8950

When McKim, Mead and White built the corner townhouse at 680 Park Avenue in 1912, it would have taken a soothsayer to predict that in the 1950s surveillance devices would be embedded in the walls, that in 1965 the building would be gutted by a developer and then dramatically saved, and that in its current life it would serve as the educational and cultural center for American relations with our neighbors north and south of the border.

A quick chronology: 1912–1948, private home; 1948–1963, the Soviet Mission (Castro and Khrushchev greet their public from the balcony); 1965, a developer buys and guts the building to erect a highrise, but after eleven days the Marquesa de Cuevas throws herself in front of the bulldozers, buys the building from the developer, and, with the help of David Rockefeller, restores it for use by the Center for Inter-American Relations, now an affiliate of the Americas Society.

The art gallery of three ground-floor rooms has four or five exhibitions each year, usually group and thematic in nature. Until recently the center mainly acted as a liaison between the United States and Latin America, and so the bulk of exhibits has been from the south: *A Century of Venezuelan Landscape Painting,*

Realism and Latin American Paintings: The 70's, Abstract Currents in Ecuadorian Art. These fine arts shows have been mixed with folk art themes—Mexican costumes and pre-Columbian pottery from Ecuador.

Now the center is also encompassing the north—Canada. In 1980 the gallery had a major exhibition of 98 artifacts from the Northwest Coast of Canada and the United States. This exhibit, like many of the others, was tied in to a series of events around the city, including films, story-telling sessions, workshops, and lectures.

The center's permanent collection of about 185 pieces can be seen throughout the building in no particular location. You can, with an appointment, take a tour upstairs, where the leaded-glass skylight, crystal chandeliers, and marble fireplaces blend surprisingly well with the Latin American art and furniture. Of particular interest is the Inca Room, with its murals of Peru as fantasized by a French artist.

Hours: Tu-Su: 12-6. Closed Christmas and New Year's Day.
Admission by donation.
Lectures and tours in English and Spanish by appointment. Picture-taking by permission.
Access: Subway: #6 to 68th Street. Bus: M1, 2, 3, 4, 101, 102. Car: Parking lots nearby.

34

Artists Space/Committee for the Visual Arts

105 Hudson Street (Franklin Street), New York, N.Y. 10013   (212) 226-3970

Having an exhibit at Artists Space is very much like an off-off Broadway run. It is a tryout for emerging artists, the big break, perhaps the first step toward stardom.

Founded in 1973 and located in large white rooms (some with unique oval windows) on the second floor of a loft building in Tribeca, Artists Space features artists who are not represented by a gallery and who have not had a solo show. Artists Space prefers to showcase talented artists at a time when their work is still raw, unresolved, and innovative; at a time when encouragement is most needed. And it likes to spot trends, to be the first on the block to know what's up and where creative sensibilities are heading.

For all of these reasons, Artists Space's exhibitions—which change about every five weeks—should not be missed by anyone interested in keeping up with what is happening in art at this moment. It is certainly one place that artists themselves visit to see what their colleagues are up to.

And young artists are up to just about everything—painting, sculpture, drawing, mixed media, performance, film, video—singly or in combination. Here are paintings inspired by the covers of pulp novels and chairs, sofas, and lamps that look like 1950s recreation-room furniture gone a little berserk. But these examples are current only at this moment, since the evolution of art is constant, and the aesthetics are diverse.

Artists Space is the visual arts program of a more broadly based group, the Committee for the Visual Arts, a service organization that provides concrete solutions to some of the difficulties faced by emerging artists. CVA gives grants to artists who need to buy materials in order to complete works in progress for planned exhibitions. Grants are also awarded to artists who want to organize their own exhibitions, and fees are given to artists who lecture at cultural and educational centers in New York State. The Unaffiliated Artists File, maintained by CVA, holds slides and résumés of 1,500 artists. These are referred to by curators, dealers, and collecters and serve as a kind of audition for an emerging artist's move to center stage.

Hours: Tu-Sa: 11-6. Closed July, August, and major holidays.
Admission free.
Lectures and tours by advance appointment.
Access: Subway: #1 to Franklin Street. Bus: M10. Car: Parking nearby.

35

Asia Society Gallery

725 Park Avenue (70th Street), New York, N.Y. 10021   (212) 288-6400

A riddle: In what society does the newly born cradle the ancient? *Answer:* At the Asia Society's elegant new headquarters, designed by contemporary architect Edward Larrabee Barnes—where extraordinary collections of Asian art are displayed in both permanent and changing exhibitions.

Dedicated in 1981, it is a rose-hued building of Regal Red granite on the outside and Indian red sandstone inside. It was built to house the society's offices and programs as well as the Mr. and Mrs. John D. Rockefeller 3rd Collection, donated in 1979 after Mr. Rockefeller's death. Since Rockefeller had been the founder of the Asia Society in 1956, as well as a longtime serious collector, his bequest was not unexpected.

Indian and Southeast Asian stone sculptures of Buddhas, deities, and human beings sit in the lobby and the second-floor Arthur Ross Gallery, a barrel-vaulted balcony and landing that leads to the Rockefeller Gallery. The gallery itself, lined with polished cherry wood cases, is purposely designed to retain an intimate quality and, therefore, is not large enough to display all of the 260 or so pieces at one time. Instead, objects are rotated so that the entire collection is exhibited within a two-year period.

This "intimate atmosphere" incorporates Mr. Rockefeller's idea of how fine collections should be shown. It seems he also had definite ideas about collecting; in fact, he would not purchase an object unless it "stirred and lifted" him. Of all the vessels, vases, scrolls, and ceramics from Afghanistan to Japan, the Rockefellers chose exquisite figures with sensitive hands (often more than two) and beatific smiles, bowls and plates with the clearest designs and glazes, birds and willows and poems on the most delicate paper. In short, a breathtaking selection.

In the former headquarters, before the permanent collection was assembled, the society had mounted 70 temporary exhibitions. In continuation of this tradition, the new ground-floor C. V. Starr Gallery now offers three or four exhibits each year that focus closely on the traditional arts of Asia. Here the visitor will find Chinese jades, Japanese paintings of tigers and lotus blossoms, Nepalese gods with numerous undulating arms, and a wide variety of other exquisite treasures.

Hours: Tu-Sa: 10-5, Th: 10-8:30, Su: 12-5. Closed Christmas and New Year's Day.
Admission fee charged.
Occasional lectures. Tours by appointment.
Access: Subway: #6 to 68th Street. Bus: M1, 2, 3, 4, 101, 102. Car: Garage parking nearby.

Aunt Len's Doll and Toy Museum

6 Hamilton Terrace (St. Nicholas Avenue and 141st Street), New York, N.Y. 10031   (212) 926-4172

Some of the dolls cry for Mama, while others rest benignly in their cradles. Some win you over by acting coy or adorable; others are sassy or sensuous. But all of the approximately 3,000 dolls—from babies to queens, from Mexican peasants to Oriental dancers—are loved and tended by their spirited collector, Lenon Holder Hoyte, a.k.a. Aunt Len.

Aunt Len's Doll and Toy Museum is in the basement of a handsome townhouse on a beautifully maintained street just one block from the City College campus. Mrs. Hoyte, a retired schoolteacher with no children of her own, began collecting dolls in 1962. Her collection is now one of the largest in the world, and she is proud to show it to visitors.

Case after case in three rooms is filled with the small people made of bisque, papier-mâché, wood, leather, fabric, celluloid, china, wax, and numerous other materials. All of the dolls are pleasing to look at, and each conducts its own history lesson. A glance at any one sets the mind reeling with memories.

Here are the Dionne quintuplets sitting in a crib, each wearing a name tag. And here is Betty Boop—no, in fact there are lots of Betty Boops in different sizes and with different expressions. Same for Shirley Temple, America's sweetheart: there are ten of her, all with the requisite dimples. Here are Howdy Doody and "product" dolls like Aunt Jemima and the Campbell Kids. And over there more contemporary figures, such as Sonny and Cher, Muhammad Ali, and John Wayne.

The international section has Middle Eastern ladies, their faces appropriately draped with veils, and colorfully dressed North and South American Indians, and recognizable replicas of our country's forefathers.

In the Collector's Room (dolls over 75 years old) you are greeted by a row of babies in carriages all lined up as if ready for their daily stroll. In one corner a tea party is actively in session, with sweet little girls each holding a stuffed pet.

Of course, no doll could live comfortably without her accessories, and Aunt Len has not ignored this detail. In addition to the dolls, she has collected their dishes, furniture, and houses. Rare books are also part of the holdings. And lest any doll find herself suddenly turned upside down, she need never worry about being embarrassed. Mrs. Hoyte makes certain that every one of her dolls is dressed—right down to her pantaloons.

Hours: By appointment: Tu-Su from 10 A.M.
    Closed major holidays and the first two weeks in August.
Admission fee charged.
Wheelchair access limited to first floor. Lectures by appointment.
Access: Subway: A, D to 145th Street. Bus: M1, 2, 3, 4, 100, 101. Car: Street parking only.

The Bartow-Pell Mansion Museum

Pelham Bay Park (Shore Road), New York, N.Y. 10464 (212) 885-1461

Hours: Tu, F & Su: 1-5. Closed occasionally in
August.
Admission fee charged.
Tours by appointment. Picture-taking by
permission.
Access: Subway and Bus: Inconvenient. Car:
Take Triborough Bridge to New England
Thruway #95. Exit at City Island/Orchard
Beach. Take Shore Road to traffic circle. Half-
way around circle, exit at sign for Pelham-
Split Rock Golf Course. Parking on premises.

The entire area of Pelham Bay Park is surprisingly suburban for New York City, even for a
section so close to the border of Westchester
County. Driving through the Bronx in the direc-
tion of City Island, first you realize that the
usual rows of buildings have been replaced by
trees. Next you spy a golf course and soon after
gates and a driveway leading to the austere but
elegant Bartow-Pell Mansion Museum.

In 1654 Thomas Pell, a colonist, bought 9,100
acres of land along Long Island Sound from the
Siwanoy Indians, with the intention of building
the Manor of Pelham. A mansion was built in
1765, housing four generations of Pells until its
destruction around the time of the Revolution.
A daughter of the fourth Lord of the Manor, Ann
Pell, married John Bartow, but the house they
built was also destroyed. Robert Bartow, a
grandson of John Bartow, built the third and
current mansion between 1836 and 1842. The
Bartows lived here until 1883, when the City of
New York bought it along with 200 acres to
create the new Pelham Bay Park.

While the city proceeded to develop the park
area, the mansion itself was neglected and fast
fell into a state of ruin until in 1914 the International Garden Club offered to restore the house
and create a formal garden. The white conservatory wing was added at this time.

The focal point of the interior is definitely the
magnificent freestanding staircase that spirals
from the spacious foyer to the attic. The rooms,
ten of them in all, are furnished primarily in
nineteenth-century American and French Empire pieces loaned by museums or privately
donated. Although the rooms are not cordoned
off with ropes or gates, the colorful patterned
carpets unfortunately have been covered in
plastic to preserve their fine condition.

The rooms are enormous and beautifully pro-
portioned with original woodwork and plaster
detailing. In the extremely large twin parlors,
elaborate doorways are decorated with carved
reliefs of eagles and cherubs, and throughout
the house ceiling fixtures are framed by plaster
medallions in leafy patterns.

A second-floor bedroom has a claw-footed
New York mahogany sleigh bed with a *cou-
ronne de lit* (bed crown) of rose-red satin lined
with gray falling in a cape behind the bed.

The formal garden extends toward Long
Island Sound, its flagstoned terraces, mani-
cured shrubs, and pool with winged nymph
creating a most appealing setting for a sunny
day's promenade.

Bedford-Stuyvesant Restoration Corporation Center

1368 Fulton Street (New York Avenue), Brooklyn, N.Y. 11216 (212) 636-3300

Much of the good news in the community of Bedford-Stuyvesant can be traced to a former milk-bottling plant on Fulton Street. That is the home of the Bedford-Stuyvesant Restoration Corporation (BSRC), an incredibly vibrant, vital multifaceted resource for the 300,000 residents of one of the nation's most severely depressed neighborhoods.

In the lobby of the BSRC and on five of its floors are changing exhibits of art. The sixth floor holds part of the small permanent collection, most of which is kept out on loan. And lest you think this functional building still resembles its industrial days, it should be noted that BSRC's lobby is a light-filled space, with brick walls and floor and potted plants that serve as a centerpiece. The other floors are bustling offices.

Exhibits, which change every four weeks, are drawn from a file of contemporary artists and from artists who approach BSRC with their portfolios. Generally the focus is on the Third World, but those boundaries have expanded. These days a visitor to BSRC may find anything from primitive art to photographs of a Yugoslavian train station taken by a black photographer to paintings from the Spirit of the Four Winds Gallery in Santa Fe, New Mexico. Work is to be found everywhere, on every floor and in almost every alcove, and visitors are free to wander through the halls and offices. Perhaps because there are so many walls to fill so frequently the art is not always of high quality. But the mediocre is more than made up for by a great find, such as photos of reggae singer Peter Tosh performing and relaxing in Jamaica.

BSRC was founded with the help of Robert Kennedy, who visited Bedford-Stuyvesant in 1966 when rioting and violence were tearing apart the already deteriorated neighborhood. Through his commitment and that of other citizens, BSRC now thrives. Its programs are both ambitious and successful—rehabilitation of nearly 400 units of housing, exterior renovation of more than 4,200 homes, construction of over 600 units of new housing, direct loans of $9 million to local businesses, and placement of over 11,000 community residents in jobs. Three newspapers, a recording studio, a legal aid department, a health-care center, a theater with both resident adult and children's companies, and other services too numerous to mention lease space in the building. Down the street from BSRC is a new shopping plaza that the corporation planned and built.

Hours: M-F: 9-5, Sa & Su: by appointment. Admission free.

Lectures and tours by appointment. Picture-taking by permission.

Access: Subway: A to Nostrand Avenue. Car: Take Williamsburg Bridge to Lee Avenue to New York Avenue. Garage parking on premises.

39

Black Fashion Museum

155 West 126th Street, New York, N.Y. 10027   (212) 666-1320

Behind the reinforced metal door of 155 West 126th Street sits a hidden heritage that will not be hidden any longer if Lois Alexander, founder and director of the Black Fashion Museum, has anything to say about it. The message of her museum is that talented black people have been designing clothes far longer and influencing fashion more profoundly than most of us realize.

The first floor of the partially renovated brownstone is devoted to exhibitions that change about every six months. When the museum opened in 1979, the first exhibit was a retrospective on contributions of blacks to fashion. Since then exhibits have included *Costumes from Black Theater, Costumes from America's Best Dressed Black Women and Men*, and *Bridal Gowns by Black Designers, 1900–1980*.

Each of the rooms on the second floor contains mannequins dressed in an eclectic assortment of costumes—day dresses and ballgowns and christening clothes. In one room there is a line-for-line reproduction of Mary Todd Lincoln's purple velvet inaugural gown (the original is in the Smithsonian), which was designed by a former slave named Elizabeth Keckley. Nearby are an authentic slave dress of finely stitched cotton and the yellow dress Rosa Parks had been sewing that day in 1955 when she changed history by refusing to give up her bus seat to a white man in Montgomery, Alabama.

Geoffrey Holder's costumes for his musical *The Wiz* strike a more fanciful note. You will see his Wizard of Oz, all in white, wearing platform shoes, and his sensuous gown for the Good Witch.

There is a costume from the show *Eubie*, designed by Bernard Johnson, and some hats can be admired that would overshadow almost any dress. Many of the clothes in the museum, however, are simply fine examples of design and craftsmanship.

One piece of information found at the Black Fashion Museum may be the best-kept fashion secret ever: It was a black woman named Ann Lowe who designed the wedding gown worn by Jacqueline Bouvier when she married John F. Kennedy.

Hours: By appointment: M-Sa: 1-8.
Admission by donation.
Access: Subway: #2, 3, A, AA, CC, D to 125th Street. Bus: M2, 7, 100, 101, 102. Car: Limited street parking and garage parking nearby.

40

The Bowne House

37-01 Bowne Street, Flushing, N.Y. 11354   (212) 359-0528

The Bowne House is one of those rare historic houses that was the site of a seminal event and remained in the same family for nine generations and therefore has many of its original furnishings.

The house was built in 1661 by John Bowne, a merchant who through marriage became a devout Quaker. He invited other Quakers to hold meetings in his kitchen and for doing so was arrested and imprisoned in 1662 by Governor Peter Stuyvesant. As an early passive resister, Bowne refused to pay the fine of 150 florins or to renounce his right to religious freedom. When imprisonment in the dungeon of the New Amsterdam fort and a diet of bread and water failed to persuade him, he was deported to Holland without his family. But in 1664 the Dutch West India Company sent him home a free man. His acquittal on the issue of religious freedom is one of the important early events that helped shape the Bill of Rights.

In 1680 John Bowne added the dining room with its pegged floor, hand-hewn beams, and handsome fireplace. One year after Bowne's death in 1695, his sixth child, Samuel, added the present entrance and parlor. A succession of Bowne descendants lived in the house until 1945, when the Bowne House Historical Society purchased it and opened it to the public.

Concern for freedom apparently was passed down through the Bowne family line, since the house served as a stop on the Underground Railroad before the Civil War. A tunnel that began between the kitchen and shed and ran for two blocks to the now-destroyed Aspinwall House has been located but not yet restored.

The house is filled with impeccably preserved furnishings, all of which were owned by the Bownes. On the wall of John Bowne's study is a Quaker marriage certificate, and on the secretary in the library is a religious text with John Bowne's name and the date 1745 written on the inside cover. The book's intimidating title: *The Memorable Works of a Son of Thunder and Consolation.*

One small room is used for rotating exhibits, ranging from early clothing to fine china.

Hours: Tu, Sa & Su: 2:30-4:30. Closed December 15 through January 15 and Easter.

Admission fee charged. School groups free by appointment.

Access: Subway: #7 to Main Street. Car: Take Triborough Bridge to Grand Central Parkway. Exit at Northern Boulevard. Turn right onto Bowne Street. Street parking nearby.

The Boxing Hall of Fame

120 West 31st Street, New York, N.Y. 10001   (212) 736-7464

If you think a museum should consist of rooms of neat exhibits creatively mounted and meticulously labeled, the Boxing Hall of Fame is not for you. But if you are a boxing buff or a fan of fabulous memorabilia and you do not mind getting your hands a little dirty, then a visit is a must.

Founded in 1954 and located on the sixth floor of a nondescript office building, the Boxing Hall of Fame is a treasure trove of boxing memories. But you will have to search a little for those memories because the place really is in disarray.

In one glass case, lying on top of one another like intimate friends, are the gloves of Jake LaMotta, Sugar Ray Robinson, Joe Frazier, Joe Louis, Floyd Patterson, and hundreds of others. Another case is filled with championship belts, huge metal things so heavily decorated with eagles and lions and gladiators that it certainly must take a champ to lift one. The walls of the one small room are lined with old color photographs of fighters with names like Kid Gavilan and Battling Levinsky.

A particularly compelling case has molds of fighters' fists—plaster casts spray-painted gold —done by a dentist who is a boxing fanatic.

"I am the paramount collector of crap," boasts Bert Randolph Sugar, the cigar-smoking owner of the Boxing Hall of Fame and its companion, *The Ring* magazine. "Who can buy a hall of fame? I can, and I did."

The Ring, confidently subtitled "The Bible of Boxing," was started in 1922 by Nat Fleischer. "He collected stuff, too," explains Sugar, which is how the Boxing Hall of Fame was born. Sugar bought all of it.

There actually is a Hall of Fame, with fighters inducted through two different methods. Modern fighters who have been retired for five years or more are elected by boxing writers from sports magazines across the country. Old-timers are brought in by a council of six men.

Such organization, and the fact that the Hall of Fame is in its thirtieth year, are proof that, despite a bit of dust and a few cartons blocking the displays, there is a method to this spirited madness and a passion for the sport of boxing.

Hours: M-F: 10-4:30. Closed major holidays.
Admission free.
Use of research facilities must be requested in writing.
Access: Subway: #1, 2, A, D, E, F to 34th Street. Bus: M1, 2, 3, 4, 5, 6, 7, 10, 16. Car: Parking lots nearby.

Bronx Museum of the Arts

851 Grand Concourse (161st Street), Bronx, N.Y. 10451 (212) 681-6000

Before May 1971 the Bronx had no art institution to call its own, no version of the Brooklyn Museum, the Queens Museum, or the Staten Island Museum, and certainly nothing like the Museum of the City of New York or the Metropolitan. But with the aid of Thomas Hoving, who was then director of the Met, the Bronx began its own program of art exhibitions, with a somewhat unusual twist—its exhibits in public spaces.

The primary exhibition space of the Bronx Museum of the Arts is located in the rotunda of the Bronx County Courthouse. It is a stately structure, typical of government buildings—marble columns, W.P.A. murals, and inspiring inscriptions high up on the walls. Centered in all this is a variety of contemporary art, from prints by an Indian printmaker to video installations.

The audience for the six or seven shows does not consist of characteristic gallery-goers, but rather courthouse employees and those people who have business in court.

In addition to the Rotunda Gallery, there are five satellite galleries located in various public places around the Bronx. These spaces are reserved for the work of Bronx-based artists from a cross section of ethnic groups. For all major exhibitions there are children's workshops and after-school and senior citizens' outreach programs.

Sometime in 1982 the museum will move to its new home, the former Young Israel Synagogue. For the first time the main gallery will not be in a spot where it is readily accessible to the public. But surely a museum that has mounted such exhibits as *The History of Comics* and *The History of the South Bronx*, aimed at showing excellent art to its community, will have no trouble drawing its patrons down the street.

Hours: M-Th: 9:30-5, Su: 12:30-4:30.
  Closed major holidays.
Admission by donation.
Tours in English and Spanish.
Access: Subway: #4, D to 161st Street.
  Car: Parking nearby.
Note: Call for updated address and hours
  information after December, 1982.

43

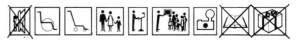

Bronx Zoo

Fordham Road at Bronx River Parkway, Bronx, N.Y. 10460 (212) 933-1759

The Bronx Zoo is to animals what the Metropolitan is to art. Ranked among the top world-class zoos, it is the biggest urban zoo in America. From its architecture to its exhibits to its breeding record, this is an impressive and fascinating place.

The Bronx Zoo cannot be seen in a single visit; with 252 acres, it simply is too sprawling. It is the kind of place you will want to revisit many times to see sections you missed on earlier trips.

The New York Zoological Park, popularly known as the Bronx Zoo, first opened its gates to the public on November 8, 1899. Over the years the exhibits of single animals in cages have been increasingly replaced by flocks and herds in complex habitats. Not only is this a more exciting way to view animals, but it also provides the best possible conditions for breeding. Today, as from the beginning, the New York Zoological Society, which operates the zoo, is concerned with field research, conservation, and protection of endangered species, as well as with exhibition.

The most historical entrance to the zoo is at its north end, through Rainey Memorial Gate and past the elaborately decorated fountain and terraces leading to the fine old buildings. Some of these buildings still house animals in cages, but they are slowly being redesigned.

To the west of the old section is the new Children's Zoo, an adventure-filled trail through a three-acre tract of natural marsh and wooded parkland. In addition to the requisite furry animals to watch and pet, there are nineteen participatory "toys" that help children understand

Hours: M-F: 10-5, Sa, Su & holidays: 10-5:30.
    November through January: 10-4:30.
Admission fee charged: F-M. Free: Tu, W & Th.
    Persons over sixty-five or under two always
    free.
Wheelchairs available by advance appointment.
Strollers for rent. Tours by appointment.
    Safari Train Tour closed November through
    January. Friends of the Zoo guided tour free
    by appointment.
Access: Subway: #2, 5 to Pelham Parkway; D
    to Fordham Road, then take BX12 bus east to
    Southern Boulevard. Car: Take Henry Hudson Parkway to Cross Bronx Expressway and
    drive east to Bronx River Parkway north.
    Take parkway to Bronx Zoo sign. Turn left
    into Bronxdale parking lot.

45

what it would be like to be an animal or a bird: tunnels to burrow through that resemble the prairie dog's home and oversized ears, like those of the fennec fox, which amplify sounds to simulate the fox's acute hearing.

One of the most exciting exhibits is *Wild Asia*, a monorail ride on the Bengali Express over the Bronx River and nearly two miles of wilderness. A tour guide points out some of the 200 specimens of mammals and birds that can be seen in this area, many of them nearly extinct—gaur (largest of the world's cattle), tahr (rugged Himalayan mountain goats), and nilghai (the largest antelope of Asia) among them.

Two other highlights, *World of Darkness,* an exhibit that reverses day and night cycles so you can see your favorite nocturnal creatures frolicking in the dark, and *World of Birds,* which presents the fabulously colored Pennent parakeet, the iridescent Tacazze sunbird, and hundreds of other winged beauties in a jungle setting, should definitely not be missed.   47

Brooklyn Botanic Garden
1000 Washington Avenue (Eastern Parkway), Brooklyn, N.Y. 11225 (212) 622-4433

In 1910 a small miracle occurred in Brooklyn which involved more than growing a tree. An ash dump on fifty acres of what is now the northeast corner of Prospect Park became the growing place for forsythia, azaleas, roses, hollies, water lilies, and about 12,000 other botanic specimens, all arranged so that a stroll at any time of year is a step into a beautifully arranged paradise.

The Brooklyn Botanic Garden describes itself as "many gardens within a garden," and this is absolutely accurate. No matter what your mood there is a spot that will suit it. A sprawling central lawn has lots of grass—splendid grass, which, wondrously, you are invited to walk on. There are trees to lie under and flowers to sniff.

The Cranford Rose Garden, nestled between the lilacs and flowering cherries, is a summer–fall feast of 5,000 bushes of more than 900 different varieties. And if you continue along, past the crab apples and herb garden, you will reach the Japanese Garden, with its shrubs rounded to suggest hillocks and clouds and its small lake filled with minnows, goldfish, and turtles.

A different kind of Japanese landscape is created in the stone garden of the Ryoanji Temple, which has no trees, bushes, or water; instead, ripple-raked crushed stones and fifteen rocks are arranged in such a way that a few minutes'

meditation refreshes the weary spirit.

Not all is nature's own at the Botanic Garden, but what's man-made is an excellent counterpart. The conservatory was built by McKim, Mead and White to hold a tropical rain forest; desert, fern, and bromeliad houses; and the country's finest bonsai collection. Stretched along the front walk are a fountain and lily pools.

Since 1914 youngsters have been growing vegetables and flowers in assigned plots in the Children's Garden. The blind have a fragrance garden, labeled for them in Braille, and all kinds of people use the reference library of 55,000 volumes. But the real centerpiece of all this is the garden itself, which is best described by the name of one water lily found there: *Gloriosa*.

Hours: April through September: Tu-F: 8-6, Sa, Su & holidays: 10-6. October through March: Closes at 4:30.
Admission free.
Lectures and tours in any language by appointment. Some restrictions on picture-taking with tripod.
Access: Subway: #2, 3 to Eastern Parkway; D, N, QB to Prospect Park. Car: Take Manhattan Bridge to Flatbush Avenue to Eastern Parkway and turn right onto Washington Avenue. Parking lot on premises.

49

The Brooklyn Children's Museum

145 Brooklyn Avenue (Saint Marks Avenue), Brooklyn, N.Y. 11213   (212) 735-4400

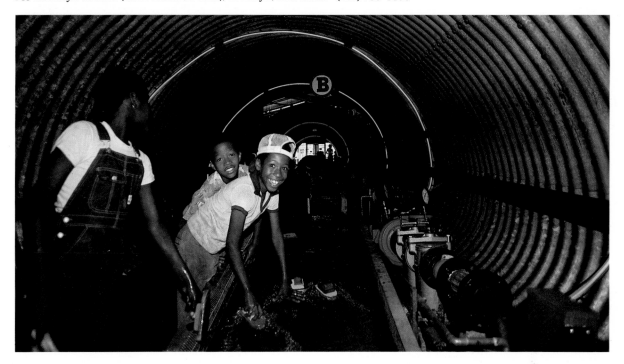

Where can you find a museum where any child "is always a welcome visitor, never an intruder"? Beyond that, a museum constructed specifically for children? In this age there are a number of museums for children, but none is as venerable as the one in the Crown Heights neighborhood of Brooklyn. The Brooklyn Children's Museum, established in 1899, was the first in the world.

The sounds, more than anything else, tell the story when you enter—laughter, chatter, and the slapping of sneakered feet heard first from the vestibule, once a 1907 trolley kiosk. The kiosk opens into a tunnel made of corrugated drainage culverts, lighted by a neon rainbow. Along one side of the tunnel a stream of water courses for the entire 180-foot length. Various exit points lead into the exhibit areas, from which the entire museum can be scanned: exposed pipes and beams, huge industrial windows, and an overall hi-tech decor.

Without being obvious in its dedication to instructing and certainly without forfeiting an atmosphere of fun, BCM's exhibits, drawn from more than 50,000 objects, teach cultural history, natural history, and technology. Their arrangement follows the classical notion of the four elements: earth, air, water, and fire.

Water, then, is that stream in the tunnel, where children float boats to figure out currents or divert the flow by making dams of rocks. Air is a hydraulic lift to ride up and down and the in-

sides of a piano to play as a harp (leading to discussions of how sound travels).

For earth, there is a greenhouse and microscopes for studying plant specimens. There are skeletons of birds, snakes, turtles, and an adolescent elephant. Nearby are minerals and fossils and small animals that have been stuffed. Fire is represented by a working steam engine.

Tucked away in odd spots are "surprise exhibits"—a case of dolls, practically at ground level; a window displaying African masks—small scenes you tend to stumble across. Much harder to miss are the two clear plastic jungle gyms, which rise in labyrinthine fashion to the ceiling. These are blowups of the molecular structure of a soap bubble and protein. Imagine viewing the world from inside a soap bubble! The Brooklyn Children's Museum makes you wish you were a kid again.

Hours: M, W, Th, F: 1-5, Sa, Su, holidays & school vacations: 10-5.

Admission free.

Participatory children's activities and general teaching collection. Wheelchair available. Picture-taking without flash permitted.

Access: Subway: #2 to Kingston Avenue; A to Kingston/Throop. Car: Take Manhattan Bridge to Flatbush Avenue to Eastern Parkway. Turn left onto New York Avenue, then right onto Saint Marks Avenue to Brooklyn Avenue. Street parking nearby.

The Brooklyn Museum

Eastern Parkway at Washington Avenue, Brooklyn, N.Y. 11238 (212) 638-5000

The Brooklyn Museum—a beautiful giant of a museum— has five floors filled with remarkable holdings from around the world. But as extensive as the Brooklyn Museum may be, it is, in fact, only one-fifth the size of its original 1893 plan. As it stands, the McKim, Mead and White structure with its domes and columns and detail work looks more like a government building that found its way from Washington, D.C., than a display place for winged genie reliefs from Assyria and drawings by Picasso. Yet, despite its size and architecture, the museum manages to be appealing and accessible, with a real community feeling.

A spin through the Brooklyn Museum (which takes all day and then only if you are moving right along) is like a world tour without need of a passport. Starting out in Africa, you bump into the Americas, and then upstairs to the serene treasures of the Orient. Upstairs again to ancient Greece, Rome, and Egypt, and then back home to the comforts of period rooms, costumes, paintings, and drawings.

Within this whirlwind are some "firsts" and "finests" worth mentioning. The Brooklyn Museum in 1923 was the first museum in the country to exhibit African objects as works of art rather than as artifacts. It has the largest and most important collection of Russian costumes and textiles outside the Soviet Union. The Egyptian collection is superb and world renowned; one startlingly fine piece is the painted wood statue *Methethy as a Mature Man*, dated about 2340 B.C., so alive it approaches portraiture. The Hudson River school of painting is particularly well represented, and the period rooms are accurate, diverse, and altogether marvelous. They are both a historian's and fantasizer's delight.

The temporary exhibitions are sometimes real blockbusters, like the show of Haitian art or Eve Arnold's photographs of China. *The Dinner Party*, Judy Chicago's sculptural feminist piece, had people lined up around the block.

Hours: W-Sa: 10-5, Su: 12-5, holidays: 1-5. Closed Christmas and New Year's Day.

Admission by donation. Children under twelve and senior citizens and members free.

Lectures and tours by appointment. Picture-taking without flash or tripod by permission.

Access: Subway: #2, 3 to Eastern Parkway/ Brooklyn Museum. Car: Take Manhattan Bridge to Flatbush Avenue to Grand Army Plaza to Eastern Parkway. Parking on premises.

Cathedral Museum

1047 Amsterdam Avenue (111th Street), New York, N.Y. 10025   (212) 678-6913

There is no mistaking the Cathedral Museum. In a thirteen-acre sea of Gothic structures, it is housed in the only one that is of Federal design. Built in the 1820s, when it served as the Leake and Watts Orphan Asylum, it predates its neighbor the magnificent Cathedral of Saint John the Divine by more than seventy years.

It seems a bit beside the point to have a special museum for a church as rich in architecture and art as Saint John the Divine, but in fact the art in the cathedral itself is considered part of the museum's domain. Under no conditions should the cathedral be missed. Its blend of Byzantine, Romanesque, and Gothic styles is wondrous.

Begin with the great bronze doors of the central portal, which in 60 panels present scenes from the Old and New Testaments. (Designed by Henry Wilson, they were cast and fabricated in Paris by Barbedienne, who also cast the Statue of Liberty.) The narthex has near the southeast side a wall of mysterious icons. Once inside, after you adjust to the overwhelming majesty and grace of the nave, walk the outer north and south aisles, where 14 bays with stained glass windows hold various kinds of art. At the east end, behind the nave, are seven chapels, also containing beautiful works.

The museum itself can be reached through a passageway at the south side of the cathedral, or you can go back outside to the building that most resembles Wall Street's Federal Hall.

Here, in a generous space two floors high and brightened by impressively tall windows, are exhibits drawn from the church's incredible art collection. A few of the most amazing works include a fourteenth-century *Annunciation* from Siena, a gentle *Madonna and Child with Saint John the Baptist* by Jacopo del Sellaio, a fifteenth-century Florentine artist; and tapestries designed for the Barberini Palace in Rome.

On the grounds there is a Biblical Garden, where flora that is mentioned in the Bible grows. An Anglican atmosphere is preserved by the attention given to such delightful details as live peacocks and well-kept lawns.

Hours: M-F: 11-4, Sa & Su: 1-4. Closed August and major holidays.

Admission free.

Wheelchairs accommodated by appointment. Lectures and tours in English, French, and Italian by advance appointment.

Access: Subway: #1, AA, B, CC to 110th Street. Bus: M4, 11, 104. Car: Parking on premises.

Center for Building Conservation

45 Peck Slip (South Street), New York, N.Y. 10038 (212) 483-0320

The Center for Building Conservation is an example of a place that takes its own advice. The advice it gives concerns the restoration and preservation of historic buildings—the very thing the center is in the process of doing to its new museum at 45 Peck Slip.

The building, the 1807 Jasper Ward counting house, had fallen into disrepair. In fact, it was collapsing. Con Edison, which owned the building, had given it to the South Street Seaport, and the Center for Building Conservation has now leased it from them. The restoration should be complete by summer 1982.

Not surprisingly, the first exhibit will be the building itself, a part of which, for purposes of comparison, will be left in its present condition. Demonstrations will show how to install a slate roof, replace rotting wood, and repair brick and brownstone—after which visitors will be able to try out their own fix-it skills. Of course there will be "before" and "after" photos of the building.

The plan is for exhibits to be the "hands-on" variety, in which sample floors and doors can be taken apart and reassembled to see how they are constructed. There will also be exhibits focusing on parts of buildings—windows, for instance—displayed to show their history and how styles and technology have developed, right up to current techniques of energy conservation.

Until the center officially opens, the staff—graduates of Columbia University's graduate program in historic preservation—will continue to work out of a second-floor loft space around the corner, at 171 John Street. Some displays can still be seen here and a visit is not unwarranted. There are cornices and joists and some windows and doors and a sincerely interested staff.

Note: Until Summer 1982 center is located at
   171 John Street. Information that follows is
   for new location. See text.
Hours: M-F: 9-5. Sa & Su: By appointment.
Admission free.
Wheelchairs accommodated on the first floor only.
Access: Subway: #2, 3, 4, 5, A, CC, J, M to
   Fulton Street. Bus: M15. Car: Parking nearby.   59

Central Park Zoo

830 Fifth Avenue (64th Street), New York, N.Y. 10021   (212) 360-8213

The zoo story in Central Park is a sad one that is getting happier. The sad part is that the country's oldest municipal zoo, which in 1873 housed 571 specimens, has become so obsolete and run-down that many of the cages are now empty and those that still have animals are more depressing than enjoyable. The happy part— and the outcome, it is hoped—is that the Department of Parks and Recreation has arranged for the New York Zoological Society to take over the Central Park Zoo and its two city-run siblings, the Prospect Park Zoo and the Queens Zoo. The New York Zoological Society, which administers the Bronx Zoo and the New York Aquarium, will renovate the three animal kingdoms, making them once again fit for beasts. It will take some time to complete this work, but in the meantime there are some attractions to take in while strolling along the east side of the park.

The first involves music and time. It is the Delacorte Musical Clock, located on the walkway between the monkey and lion houses. Instrument-playing beasts surround the clock, and two monkeys sit above, ready to strike the bell. On the hour and the half-hour the carillon chimes and the animals go to work. All in a circle, they play their instruments and dance to the pretty tune. The elephant is on the accordion, the bear on the tambourine, and the baby kangaroo, along with its mother, plays the horn. Alas, even the mechanical has its problems at the zoo. The clock is often out of whack because, it seems, urine fumes from the monkey house corrode the mechanism.

The other highlight is a gorilla born at the Central Park Zoo on September 3, 1972, to parents Lulu and Kongo. The birth of this baby caused such a stir that the *Daily News* sponsored a naming contest. From among thousands of submissions, one, from a Staten Island fire fighter who wanted to honor his wife, Patricia, was selected. The winning name: Patty Cake. And she continues to charm New York. The faithful visit her daily—not only children but gorilla-loving adults, who wave and coo and say such things as "Patty Cake, did you miss me? I'm sorry I was late today. Patty Cake, sweetheart, are you angry with me?"

The Children's Zoo is a particularly good place to spend an afternoon with the kids.

Hours: Buildings: Daily: 11-5. Outside area:
 Always open. Children's Zoo: Daily: 10-5.
Admission free. Children's Zoo: Small fee charged.
Wheelchair access ramp at 66th Street entrance.
 Tours in the Old Dairy Building. Picture-
 taking with tripod preferred 8-11 A.M. only.
Access: Subway: RR to 5th Avenue. Bus: M1, 2,
 3, 4. Car: Parking difficult.

61

China Institute in America

125 East 65th Street, New York, N.Y. 10021 (212) 744-8181

Hours: M-F: 10-5, Sa: 11-5, Su: 2-5. Closed major holidays and between exhibitions. Call before visiting.

Admission by donation.

Lectures and tours in English and Chinese. Tours in other languages may be arranged. Picture-taking by permission.

Access: Subway: #4, 5, N, RR to 59th Street; #6 to 68th Street. Bus: M15, 29, 101. Car: Garage parking and limited street parking nearby.

It is a handsome but not unusual townhouse on Manhattan's Upper East Side except for one small but undeniable detail—the two fearsome stone monsters that flank the stoop. These are the protectors of the China Institute in America and its exhibition space, the China House Gallery.

The institute, formed in 1926 by a group of Chinese and American educators, has a long record of community service and cultural and educational programs for Chinese immigrants, Chinese-Americans, and the general public.

The gallery is in what once was the drawing room of this townhouse, a small yet comfortable space. Twice a year—from the end of October to the end of January and from the end of March to the end of May—exhibitions are mounted on a particular aspect of the Chinese culture's extensive arts: the intricate embroidery of Imperial China, precious and surprisingly detailed miniatures, luxurious silk tapestries, sensuous Tantric Buddhist art. At times special themes have been chosen—gardens, landscapes, dragons, and even the portrayal of foreigners in Chinese art. Then there have been East-meets-West shows, such as *Chinese Porcelains in European Mounts* and *China's Influence on American Culture in the 18th and 19th Centuries*. Whatever the theme, the exhibitions are of the finest quality and quite extensive for a gallery of this size.

And if you're wondering how the gallery works out its role with Taiwan and the People's Republic, you'll discover that both are recognized: representatives from each country are invited to major activities.

For six weeks during the summer, the China House Gallery concentrates on a folk art. One year it might be lanterns, another year toys, and the year after that the beautiful knots used to decorate objects and clothing. Workshops are held during this time for those who want to learn the craft.

The yard of the townhouse, which is open to the public, is a lovely Chinese garden that, although nothing like the Metropolitan's Astor Court, is planted with trees and shrubs indigenous to China.

Chinese Museum

8 Mott Street (Chatham Square), New York, N.Y. 10013   (212) 964-1542

To get to the Chinese Museum, enter the China-town arcade at 8 Mott Street, walk past the deafening assortment of computer games with names such as Space Invaders and Pac Man, past the Dancing Chicken (a live chicken that, for 50 cents, will scratch the floor with a dance-like motion and then dive for a sprinkling of food), and go directly to the change booth. Tell the proprietor that you want to see the Chinese Museum. He will direct you up a flight of back stairs, sending along an employee to unlock the door. He might also yell out, "Don't forget to show them the dragon."

The dragon turns out to be a fake monstrosity in a display case that, not unlike the live chick-en, will wag its tail and stick out its tongue for 25 cents. That is where the similarity between downstairs and upstairs ends.

Other displays in the one dimly lit room somehow manage to convey calm and dignity. Calligraphy, incense, China's contribution to civilization (noodles, paper, dice, the abacus), and the symbolic meaning of flowers in paint-ing, poetry, and ceremonies are all rather sen-sitively described through examples and ex-planations. A large gold Buddha rests on an or-nate altar. A red rickshaw sits in the center of the room.

All the while, the floor boards rattle with the cacophony of battles between man and ma-chine taking place below. A large replica of Con-fucius sits behind smeared glass and silently appraises the whole situation.

Hours: Daily: 10-6.
Admission fee charged.
Tours for 25 or more by appointment.
Access: Subway: #36, J, RR to Canal Street.
  Bus: M1, 15, 101, 102. Car: Metered street
  parking and lot parking nearby.

63

Chung-Cheng Art Gallery

Sun Yat-sen Hall, St. John's University, Jamaica, N.Y. 11439   (212) 990-6161, extension 6582

What is this structure that appears to be a Chinese temple on the campus of a Catholic university? It is the golden pagoda, Sun Yat-sen Hall, St. John's Center for Asian Studies.

The exterior of the building is yellow brick with a red and gold roof carved with a variety of demons. In the lobby, center stage, is an intimidating statue of Sun Yat-sen, the founder of the Republic of China.

Display cases line the walls here and along a hallway leading into the Chung-Cheng Art Gallery (the name was chosen to honor the memory of Chiang Kai-shek, whose official name was Chiang Chung-Cheng). It is a fairly modest room with 1,000 fabulous objects that are anything but modest.

There is a samurai sword and a number of sword guards of gold inlay, bronze, and cloisonné in the form of fish, generals, sages, and landscapes. There are delicate blue and white porcelain and cloisonné plates, and brush pots of iron, bamboo, jade, and porcelain. There is a lacquerware writing box with a gold inlayed cover and gold powder sprinkled inside and on the instruments. In contrast there is the pure white porcelain figure of Kwannon, the Japanese goddess of mercy, with her delicate expression and hands. There are beautifully glazed vases, and ivory carvings that look as ephemeral as clouds. Perhaps the most fabulous in the least obvious way is an ink set made as a tribute to Emperor K'ang-hsi (1662–1722).

Along two walls and in the center of the gallery on movable racks is space for changing exhibitions. These shows, mounted eight times a year, are generally the work of contemporary Asian artists, many of whom are having their first exhibits in this country.

Despite the building's Chinese decor, half of the collection is from Japan. When the collection was started (with a sizable donation of artifacts from the 1964 World's Fair), the pieces were exhibited in the library. At the suggestion of the librarian, the Asian Studies Department found its own place to put their things, which is how the golden pagoda came to be.

Hours: Daily: 10-8. Closed Thanksgiving. Admission free.

Lectures in English and Chinese by appointment. Tours and research facilities available by appointment.

Access: Subway and Bus: E or F train to Kew Gardens, then transfer to Q44A bus to 173rd Street/Union Turnpike. Car: Take Queens-Midtown Tunnel to Long Island Expressway. Exit at Utopia Parkway, then go south on Utopia Parkway, past Union Turnpike. The campus is on the right. Parking available.

City Gallery

2 Columbus Circle, New York, N.Y. 10019   (212) 974-1150

Some people still call the white marble building with the round windows on the south side of Columbus Circle the Huntington Hartford Museum. But Mr. Hartford's gallery of modern art was not a success, and the art shown today at 2 Columbus Circle is on the second floor only, where the City Gallery mounts exhibits relating to the City of New York.

The rest of the building is occupied by the City's Department of Cultural Affairs, the National Endowment for the Arts' regional office, and the New York Convention and Visitor's Bureau, which maintains a staffed information table and racks of brochures in the lobby.

Opened in October 1980, City Gallery is dedicated to art that is about our metropolis and its diverse communities. The exhibitions are curated by nonprofit arts organizations from the five boroughs.

City Gallery particularly likes to accept the kind of exhibit that gives nonprofit arts groups from other boroughs and neighborhoods an opportunity to receive exposure in midtown Manhattan. The idea is that after viewers see the exhibits they will visit the places themselves, thus expanding their geographical and cultural knowledge. One such exhibit was a survey of alternative art spaces located throughout lower Manhattan.

Another kind of exhibit celebrates and illuminates various aspects of life in New York. Work by Hispanic artists and the Children's Art Carnival are examples. A less joyous but nonetheless real aspect of urban life—homeless women, also known as shopping bag ladies—was the focus of a photography exhibit.

Hours: M-F: 10-5:30.
Admission free.
Access: Subway: #1, A, AA, B, CC, D to 59th
   Street. Bus: M10, 103, 104. Car: Garage
   parking nearby.

The City Island Historical Nautical Museum

190 Fordham Street, City Island, Bronx, N.Y. 10464   (212) 885-1292

The City Island Historical Nautical Museum feels a bit like a tour of grandmother's attic, which in fact it very much is. The museum's objects—nautical and historical artifacts pertaining to City Island—have been donated by residents of the island, many of whose families have lived here for generations.

The museum itself is housed in three rooms of the old schoolhouse, P.S. 17, built after the 1895 elections, when the residents of City Island voted to separate from West Chester County and become part of the Bronx. That vote went through at least partially because the politicians had promised the citizens a new bridge and school if they seceded.

The museum, staffed entirely by volunteers, is set up not unlike a school exhibit. Objects are hung from the walls and neatly set up in display cases. Labels are carefully written in block print. To get from one room to the next you walk down a hall, past low drinking fountains, feeling as if you are about to be stopped because you don't have a permission pass.

The Walsh Room is so named because it contains 62 paintings of City Island scenes done in the 1930s by Harold Vandervoort Walsh, a local artist and professor of architecture at Columbia University. Also in this room are Indian arrowheads, paint pots, and pounding tools found on or near the island.

The Nautical Room focuses on City Island's maritime history, both in wartime and in peace. There are construction and launching photographs of America's Cup defenders built on City Island, plus other intriguing memorabilia that includes a painted plate from the *Lusitania* and a wooden chain carved by a sailor from a single piece of wood so that it has no beginning or end.

The Home Community Room is filled with interesting ephemera—citizenship papers from the 1800s, Dr. F. E. Lawrence's bill of $15 for the delivery of a baby, a funeral bill from 1906 for $116.25, and a butcher's account book from 1905 that shows beef selling for 18 cents a pound. Beautiful white dresses hang in the closets, along with a kimono brought back from the Orient by a sea captain.

Hours: Su: 2-4. Weekdays by appointment.
Admission free.
Occasional lectures. Picture-taking with flash by permission.
Access: Subway and Bus: #6 train to Pelham Bay Park, then take #12 bus to City Island. Car: Take FDR Drive north to Bruckner Expressway to Hutchinson River Parkway to City Island exit. Follow signs to City Island. At third light after bridge turn left onto Fordham Street. Parking nearby in rear yard.

The Clocktower/The Institute for Art and Urban Resources

108 Leonard Street (Broadway), New York, N.Y. 10013 (212) 233-1096

Hours: W-F: 1-6, Sa: 10-6. Closed July through September and major holidays.
Admission by donation.
Occasional talks given by artists on their work. Tours by appointment. Picture-taking by permission.
Access: Subway: #6, A, AA, CC, E, RR to Canal Street. Bus: M1, 6. Car: Parking difficult.

At the point where Broadway meets Leonard Street and Catherine Lane a four-faced clock in a wonderful-looking tower chimes the time on the hour. The towered building stands alone, a rare sight in this crowded metropolis.

Designed by the firm of McKim, Mead and White and constructed for the New York Life Insurance Company around 1912, this magnificent structure is now owned by the City of New York, which uses it for courtrooms and offices. Sanitation, probation, and various other municipal departments are housed on the first twelve floors. On the thirteenth floor and in the tower, along with the clock's mechanism, is a unique arts space appropriately known as the Clocktower.

That an arts space ended up in such an unlikely spot can be attributed to the efforts of Alanna Heiss, the energetic founder and director of the Institute for Art and Urban Resources, which operates both the Clocktower and Project Studios One in Long Island City, Queens. Heiss began salvaging abandoned buildings in 1971 for artists' work spaces and exhibitions. But what she really wanted was a permanent exhibition place located high up in the city's landscape. One day she spied the clocktower.

Before the spring of 1973 when the Clocktower opened, the thirteenth floor was used as a storehouse for war rations. Once the cartons of old food were lugged away, a lovely gallery space emerged, easily reached by taking the elevator to the twelfth floor and walking up one flight. One more flight up is another room, square with a very high ceiling and a winding silvery steel staircase that leads to the clock's mechanism and a balcony that affords a fantastic 360-degree view.

The Clocktower mounts in-depth one-person exhibitions, often featuring artists whose careers are just emerging. Sixteen shows are scheduled each year, and part of the space is annually awarded to an artist to use as a studio. The exhibits are either guest curated or accepted through proposals submitted by artists to the Institute for Art and Urban Resources. As at P.S. 1, the unexpected can be expected.

And just as the old clocktower has been given a new life, so has the clock itself. Prior to 1980 it had not worked for at least twenty years. Two city employees, Eric Reiner and Marvin Schneider, worked during their lunch hours and days off for more than a year to restore the clock, and they still come by regularly to check and set it.

The Cloisters

Fort Tryon Park (near 190th Street), New York, N.Y. 10040 (212) 923-3700

When you sit in the Bonnefont Cloister with the sunlight warming your face and the rich harmonies of Gregorian chants washing over you, tense muscles begin to relax and your mood slowly mellows and you cannot imagine why coming here is not a regular part of your life.

Along with the Frick, the Cloisters is one of New York's rare spots of tranquillity. Located high above Manhattan and overlooking the Hudson, it is a medieval-style structure that incorporates sections from such monuments as a twelfth-century chapter house, parts of cloisters from five medieval monasteries, a Romanesque chapel, and a twelfth-century Spanish apse. Such a mix could be rather jarring, but fortunately the effect here is quite the opposite. As soon as you spy this castlelike edifice set in Fort Tryon Park and then walk up the long flight of steps, you feel as if no harm can come to you.

What is a cloister anyway? It is the enclosed courtyard of a monastery and its surrounding arcaded walkway. True to its name, the Cloisters has more than one—in fact four, each quite different from the next. The Cuxa Cloister is pink marble glowing against green grass. The Trie Cloister looks toward the George Washington Bridge, and has an herb garden and espaliered fruit trees. The Saint-Guilhem Cloister has a palm tree and paneless, arched windows, and the Bonnefont Cloister is often filled with music.

But there is much more to the Cloisters than cloisters. There is magnificent art. Here is where you will find the stunning Unicorn Tapestries; incredible tomb effigies of thirteenth- and fourteenth-century nobility, fully clothed and resting peacefully; stonework, woodwork, and stained glass that have been crafted with the greatest precision; and glorious religious paintings and sculpture.

The Cloisters is a branch of the Metropolitan Museum of Art and was made possible through the munificence of John D. Rockefeller, Jr.

Hours: Tu-Sa: 10-4:45, Su & holidays: 1-4:45, except May through September, Su: 12-4:45. Closed major holidays.

Admission fee charged.

Wheelchairs accommodated by advance notice. Tours and research facilities available by appointment. Picture-taking without flash or tripod permitted.

Access: Subway: A to 190th Street, then walk through the park. Bus: M4. Car: Take Henry Hudson Parkway to Cloisters exit. Free parking on premises.

69

Con Edison Energy Museum

145 East 14th Street, New York, N.Y. 10003   (212) 460-6244

What happens when you switch on a light? What makes the subway rumble by? What does a New York electrician see when he slips down into a manhole? In the dusky maze that is the Con Edison Energy Museum such mysteries are revealed.

The exhibition is the type of technologically sleek display we grew accustomed to at the 1964 New York World's Fair—a path that winds enough to cause small thrills of anticipation at every turn; and windows that light up and voices that speak when you press red buttons.

The energy tour begins with the electric arc lamp and Thomas Edison's invention of the incandescent light, the first of which burned for 40 hours. Edison devised not only the electric light but the entire New York power system as well. On September 4, 1882, the power at Edison Central Station at 257 Pearl Street (now a parking lot) was switched on, and to prove it worked Edison himself flipped on a lamp at J. P. Morgan's residence uptown. On that day 400 lamps were lit.

The "Century of Progress" section of the museum illustrates the rapid growth of electrical technology and its impact on the home, factory, and office. Motors and drills, fans and toasters, a washing machine and a coffee perculator, a Singer sewing machine and an Edison ediphone (an early dictating machine) are shown.

From that kitchen of sixty years ago it is a fairly wide leap into "Underground New York," the highlight of the museum. A passageway built in the shape of a large manhole takes you into a cavernlike room that simulates what is beneath a city street. Here a fantastic, colorful, pulsing, audiovisual presentation describes the routes of electric, gas, water, telephone, steam, and sewer lines. The sound of a subway rushing by completes the underground scenario.

The museum maze ends with "Energy Sources for the Future," which is concerned with current research efforts in solar energy, liquefaction of coal, a new high-voltage transmission system, and the generation of electricity from the space-age fuel cell.

Found uptown on the street level of the Chrysler Building is the Con Edison Conservation Center, a veritable idea bank of tips on how to conserve energy and lower bills. The tips offered in this exhibition are well worth noting, since they are the extent of what Con Edison gives free to its customers.

Hours: Tu-Sa: 10-4. Closed major holidays.
Admission free.
Lectures and tours in English, Spanish, and
    German.
Access: Subway: #4, 6, LL, N, RR to Union
    Square/14th Street. Bus: M9, 14, 101, 102.
    Car: Parking lot nearby.

Con Edison Conservation Center

405 Lexington Avenue, New York, N.Y. 10174
(212) 599-3435

Hours: M-Sa: 10-5:30. Closed some major
    holidays.
Admission free.
Group tours by appointment. Picture-taking by
    permission.
Access: Subway: #4, 5, 6, 7 to Grand Central/
    42nd Street; Bus: M101, 102, 104; Car: Garage
    parking nearby.

The Conference House

Conference House Park (Hylan Boulevard and Satterlee Street), Staten Island, N.Y. 10307   (212) 984-2086

With its front lawn rolling down to Raritan Bay and its view of pretty sailboats docked at the yacht club at Perth Amboy, the Conference House is set on a choice piece of land, once part of the 1,600 acres granted in 1687 to a colonist named Christopher Billop.

The house itself, a stone manor, was built around 1680. The Billop family lived there until after the Revolution when Christopher's great-grandson, also named Christopher, suffered the same fate as a good many Tories: his home and land were confiscated, and he was forced to leave the country. He chose to move to Canada.

But before the end of the war a meeting took place at the Billop estate that was important enough to change the home's name to the Conference House.

The Battle of Long Island had taken place and the British were in control of New York. Yet, the Declaration of Independence had been signed on July Fourth in Philadelphia, and the Colonists were not about to surrender. Admiral Lord Howe, the British commander, called for a meeting with the Americans. So on September 11, 1776, Benjamin Franklin, John Adams, and Edward Rutledge, having traveled from Philadelphia to Perth Amboy, took a barge across to the Billop place and met there with Lord Howe. Of course, Howe's attempt to stop the War of Independence failed.

The furnishings in the house today were not owned by the Billops, whose belongings were either sold or were moved with the family to Canada. But the house is furnished authentically for the 1750s. On the first floor is the parlor where the historic conference was held; across from it is the formal dining room. The second floor has two very large bedrooms and a small room outfitted as a study. The kitchen is typically in the basement, and today it really is the center of the house. It is a working kitchen that is used on the first Sunday of every month for cooking and baking.

Hours: W-Su: 1-5. Closed major holidays.
Admission fee charged.
Wheelchairs accommodated by advance appointment. Lectures and tours by appointment.
Access: Subway to Ferry: #1 to South Ferry; #4, 5 to Bowling Green; N, RR to Whitehall Street. Bus to Ferry: M1, 6, 15. After Ferry: Staten Island Rapid Transit Train: To Tottenville; Bus: #103 to Carteret. Car: Turn left onto Bay Street, then right onto Hylan Boulevard to the end. Parking on premises.

Cooper-Hewitt Museum
The Smithsonian Institution's National Museum of Design
Fifth Avenue at 91st Street, New York, N.Y. 10028   (212) 860-6868

Hours: Tu: 10-9, W-Sa: 10-5, Su: 12-5. Closed
   major holidays.
Admission fee charged, except Tuesdays, 5-9.
Lectures in some foreign languages depending
   on exhibit. Courses, lectures, and tours for
   adults and young people. Picture-taking
   without flash or tripod permitted. Library and
   other research facilities available by
   appointment.
Access: Subway: #4, 6 to 86th Street. Bus: M1,
   2, 3, 4. Car: Garage parking nearby.

The entire focus of the Cooper-Hewitt Museum
is the way we live—our dishes and silverware,
our wallpaper and furniture, our architecture
and fashions. Embroidery, lace, metalwork,
woodwork, glass, textiles, and all the stuff of
homes can be found in the Cooper-Hewitt's collections.

Originally called the Cooper Union Museum
for the Arts of Decoration, it was established in
1897 by Sarah, Eleanor, and Amy Hewitt,
granddaughters of Peter Cooper. Cooper was the
man who generously founded the Cooper Union
for Advancement of Science and Art, a tuition-
free school that still operates today. The
museum had been a part of his vision, but he
did not have the funds to begin it. Instead, his
granddaughters fulfilled the dream.

But the pleasure of sampling the museum's
treasures was almost lost awhile ago. In 1963
the trustees of the Cooper-Hewitt (the museum's administrators then) found the museum
too costly and closed it. A committee to save the
museum was formed, and in 1967 the Smithsonian Institution assumed the administrative
responsibility. In 1976 the Cooper-Hewitt
reopened in the former Andrew Carnegie Mansion, a home that epitomizes one aspect of
American design—Fifth Avenue's magnate
mansions.

The mansion serves as a splendid home for
the Cooper-Hewitt's extensive collections of
design and decorative arts, which total 300,000
objects from all parts of the world and from
every historical period covering a span of 3,000
years.

Although some of the rooms have been
renovated in a rather nondescript manner, certain parts of the mansion—particularly the
main stairway and rooms on the ground
floor—retain their original luxurious atmosphere.

The exhibitions, which change regularly,
cover a fascinating range—from set and
costume designs of nineteenth-century German
theater productions to a documentation of the
suburbs, from a survey of animated film techniques to a study of gardens and their uses in
our lives.

The library of 35,000 volumes, picture archives containing 2 million items, and educational programs for adults and young people
round out the Cooper-Hewitt's services and
bring new vitality to the Carnegie Mansion.

The Drawing Center
137 Greene Street (Houston Street), New York, N.Y. 10012   (212) 982-5266

By 1977 curator Martha Beck had observed two things about the art market: that drawings were not considered a commercial or central priority of art institutions; and that young artists had no regular place to show their drawings. So she opened the Drawing Center on the ground floor of an 1887 cast-iron building in Soho, and since then she has run it with the absolute clarity and forthrightness with which it was begun.

The Drawing Center's selection process is definitely a case of "many come but few are chosen." Each year Beck and her staff look at the work of some 1,400 artists, and they give advice on career options and dealers and where the artists might try next. The artists' slides and résumés are placed in the archives (a file that now contains about 2,500 names), which is then used by dealers, curators, collectors, and other artists. But of the 1,400 who come to the center throughout the year, only 50 artists are asked to exhibit in one of the four annual group shows.

In order to exhibit at the Drawing Center, artists cannot be connected with a dealer or have had a solo show. As a result of exhibiting at the Drawing Center, however, many artists have moved quickly into the commercial marketplace.

There is also one thematic show during the year: in 1980 it was manuscripts documenting the diverse and often quirky methods that composers such as Mozart, Haydn, Brahms, John Cage, Philip Glass, and Steve Reich have used to represent musical sounds; in 1981 it was sculptors' drawings from 1400 to 1950. Lectures, concerts, or other events complementing the exhibitions are held in the gallery, as are programs on the care and conservation of works on paper.

Hours: M-Sa: 11-6, W: 11-8. Closed major holidays and the first two weeks in September.
Admission free.
Lectures for schoolchildren in English, Chinese, and Spanish. Picture-taking without flash permitted.
Access: Subway: #6 to Broadway/Lafayette Street; A, E to Houston Street; RR to Prince Street. Bus: M5, 10, 21. Car: Parking nearby.

Dyckman House Museum

4881 Broadway (204th Street), New York, N.Y. 10034   (212) 397-3084

On a high rise of land across the street from a gas station at the busy intersection of 204th Street and Broadway is a pretty eighteenth-century Dutch Colonial farmhouse, the only remaining farmhouse in Manhattan. At one time the Dyckman farm was 300 acres, with fruit trees sloping down to the Harlem River. Even as late as 1904 there were apple trees thriving on what is today the IRT subway line.

The house of wood, brick, and stone has a front porch, a gambrel roof, Dutch double doors, and a large backyard with ivy, shrubs, a well, and the last existing peach tree from the original orchards. Built around 1783, it is on the site of an earlier Dyckman house that burned during the Revolutionary War. Rather than being lavish like the Morris-Jumel or Van Cortlandt mansions, it is a good-sized but practical home of two floors and a kitchen in the basement. A cutaway in the right wall of the entrance hall shows details of the house's construction—handhewn studs and laths held together with homemade nails and fillings of mud and marsh grass. (Marsh grass! Incredible to imagine a marsh in this area.)

Unfortunately, none of the artifacts or period furnishings are labeled in any detail, but the rooms are pleasant, particularly the colonial kitchen where you can find a spinning wheel, a pine hutch, caldrons, a Dutch oven, and a long-handled coffee roaster and waffle iron.

The Relics Room has artifacts from revolutionary campsites and area farms, such as fragments of Dutch tiles, cutlery, buckles, horseshoes, solid shot, and bullets, including one supposedly chewed by a prisoner while he was being lashed.

The house, slated for demolition in 1915, was saved by two Dyckman descendants, who restored and donated it to the City of New York, which still administers it.

Hours: Tu-Su: 9-5. Closed major holidays.
Admission free.
Lectures by two-week advance appointment.
 Tours in English and Spanish.
Access: Subway: #1, A to Dyckman Street. Bus: M104 to 125th Street, then transfer to M5 to 168th Street, then transfer to M100. Car: Metered street parking nearby.

Edgar Allan Poe Cottage

East Kingsbridge Road and Grand Concourse, Bronx, N.Y. 10458   (212) 881-8900

The life of Edgar Allan Poe, it seems, was no less tortured than that of his characters. This talented poet and fiction writer was an orphan who as an adult drank, took drugs, had breakdowns, and ultimately died of severe exposure during a drinking binge at the age of 40, two years after the death of his beloved wife, Virginia.

The place where Poe lived from 1846 until his death in 1849 is on the edge of a leisure park on the Grand Concourse in the Bronx. It is a pretty, white shingle and clapboard farmer's cottage he rented from the Valentine family for 100 dollars a year. The park was once a cherry orchard in the area known as Fordham Village. The Poe Cottage is noteworthy not only because it is where the author spent his last years but also because it is the only structure left among the original 34 village buildings, which included a blacksmith, a hotel, and two taverns.

When Poe moved here in 1846, his wife, who was also his first cousin, was dying of tuberculosis. Poe had married Virginia Clemm when he was 27 and she a mere 13. Details of her death are curiously coincidental with other key events in Poe's life. For example, Virginia died on January 30, 1847 (the same month and day that Poe's brother William Henry had been born), at the age of 24 (the same age at which both his mother and William Henry died).

Poe's own descriptions of his cottage have been followed to re-create the interior so that it looks as sparse as it did when he lived there. Two pieces of furniture were actually owned by Poe: the rocking chair, which sits near the fireplace in the sitting room/study, and the bed, in the claustrophobic first-floor room where Virginia died. Overall the house is only five tiny, low-ceilinged rooms, four of which are open to the public.

It was in these spartan quarters that Poe wrote such great works as "Annabel Lee."

Hours: W-F: 1-5, Sa: 10-4, Su: 1-5. Closed
   Christmas and New Year's Day.
Admission fee charged.
Picture-taking by permission. Research facilities:
   See Museum of Bronx
   History/Valentine-Varian House.
Access: Subway: #4, D to Kingsbridge Road.
   Car: Take Major Deegan Expressway to Fordham Road exit, then go east to Grand Concourse and north to Kingsbridge Road. Street parking nearby.

Fashion Moda

2803 Third Avenue (147th Street), Bronx, N.Y. 10455 (212) 585-0135

According to the definition the directors of Fashion Moda put forth in the January 1981 issue of *Artforum*, "Fashion Moda is impossible to define because by definition we have no definition." Yet within this lack of structure there emerges a philosophy that goes something like this: Fashion Moda believes in the idea that art can be made by people who are known and unknown, trained and untrained, middle class and poor. It is paint applied to canvas and then carefully framed. It is graffiti scrawled across walls. It is the cross-cultural concept that all people are one and the same, a theory that the directors hope will ripple out from the New York community, into the national community and, subsequently, into the world. Fashion Moda would like to be a franchise.

Fashion Moda is a place for science, invention, technology, art, and fantasy. Its proper name is the word *fashion* written in the four languages —English, Chinese, Spanish, and Russian— that are spoken by a large portion of the world's population. The word itself was chosen because fashion always reflects its immediate environment and is in itself a mannerism.

Fashion Moda's base of operations since 1978 has been a storefront in the South Bronx, a neighborhood described as "an area of severe devastation," but one that Fashion Moda sees as crucial for implementing their idea and escaping the chic art scene.

But the storefront isn't the only spot where Fashion Moda exhibits art. It likes, for example, to "borrow" abandoned buildings.

The storefront itself might be the scene of *City Maze*, a labyrinth built throughout the entire room by two artists. Or *The Hall of Fame*, face castings of neighborhood people. Or *Animals Living in Cities*, a group show that included work about wild dogs in India, rats in Italy, black widow spiders in Atlanta, and a wealth of information about New York's own uninvited roommates—cockroaches, rats, and mice.

So in keeping with its defiance of definition, Fashion Moda's exhibitions defy classification. Except perhaps to note that they are beyond even what alternative museums are showing and they might turn up almost anywhere.

Hours: Tu-Sa: 2-7. Closed major holidays.
Admission free.
Lectures and tours by advance appointment.
Access: Subway: #2, 5 to 3rd Avenue/149th
  Street. Car: Parking nearby.

81

Federal Hall National Memorial
26 Wall Street (Nassau Street), New York, N.Y. 10005 (212) 264-8711

Hours: M-F: 9-5. Closed major holidays, except
   Memorial Day, Fourth of July, and
   Washington's birthday.
Admission free.
Occasional lectures. Brochures available in
   English, French, German, Spanish, Chinese,
   Japanese, and Italian.
Access: Subway: #2, 3, 4, 5, N, RR to Wall
82   Street. Bus: M6, 15. Car: Parking lots nearby.

Federal Hall, with its statue of George Washington gazing down Broad Street, is one of New York's most illustrious buildings. The current structure, completed in 1842, resembles Athens's Parthenon, with its Doric columns and triangular pediment, but the events that have taken place on this site constitute a lesson in only one country's history—America's.

Federal Hall is where the government of the United States, under our present Constitution, began to operate on March 4, 1789. New York City was the first capital and Federal Hall the first capitol. Eight weeks after Congress met here for its first session, George Washington, standing on the balcony, took the oath of office, while excited New Yorkers looked on from the street and rooftops.

Before the site became Federal Hall, it was the location of New York's City Hall. There, in 1765, delegates representing nine of the colonies met to draw up a petition against Parliament's Stamp Act. The Stamp Act Congress taught the colonies how to unite politically and was a harbinger of the revolution to come.

The current structure served first as a U.S. Customs House. Later, as a branch of the Independent Treasury System, it was the repository for 70 percent of the Federal government's revenues.

Federal Hall today is administered by the National Park Service, which has organized honest, interesting exhibits. The models, pictures, and clearly written text give a feeling not only of Federal Hall's history but of what eighteenth-century New York was like.

Those who pine for a simpler, more charming life would do well to view the exhibit to the right of the rotunda. It realistically describes Colonial life, including noise and water pollution. The room to the left of the rotunda commemorates Washington's inauguration.

Two rooms on the second floor house additional exhibits. One describes the first freedom-of-press trial, that of John Peter Zenger, publisher of the outspoken New York *Weekly Journal*, who was formally accused of "seditious libel," locked up in the City Hall jail for nine months before being found not guilty.

The second exhibit, called *Ever Changing, Ever Free,* is a tribute to the Bill of Rights. Video monitors, dotting the room at various angles and heights, show a continuous film on contemporary applications of freedom of speech, press, worship, and the other protections assured by the Bill of Rights.

Ferkauf Museum of the International Synagogue

John F. Kennedy International Airport, Jamaica, N.Y. 11430   (212) 656-5044

Opposite the International Arrivals Building, near parking lots 2 and 4, beneath the traffic patterns of arriving and departing planes are three houses of God sitting side by side—Catholic, Protestant, and Jewish. This is the Tri-Faith Plaza of John F. Kennedy International Airport.

The International Synagogue is particularly worth noting because of its architectural features and its museum. The synagogue itself is a three-story-high room with huge stone tablets at the ark on which there are reliefs by contemporary artist Chaim Gross depicting the Ten Commandments. On either side and above the ark are stained glass windows in an abstract blue and rose pattern, like the sky at sunrise.

In an adjoining room is the Ferkauf Museum, filled with gifts from Jewish communities throughout the world. The first thing you see when you enter the room is a framed page written in Hebrew. It is a passage—handwritten from memory by a man in a concentration camp—from the Talmud, the compilation of Jewish laws, ethics, history, and sermonic material. Other objects include an ark containing three Torahs—one from Ellis Island, one from Germany, and one from Rumania. The German Torah had been buried in a Berlin cemetery during the Nazi era. The Torah from Rumania was supposedly tossed into the air by

some Nazis who were playing with the religious object; it landed in a chandelier and was left there, which is how it survived the Holocaust.

There is also a Yemen bridal set consisting of a colorful headdress, sandals, a handbag, and a ketubah (marriage contract); a small ark from Thailand; an Eternal Light from Bucharest; Torah pointers from Portugal and Italy; and many pieces from India, including a contemporary book rest and two silver Torah cases that were made in Persia but used in India.

The collection numbers around 300 objects, but because the room is not large enough to display all of the pieces at once, they are rotated. Yet, no matter what is on view, the museum is always filled with precious reminders to the Jewish people that their religion is internationally observed.

Hours: Su-F: 9-5. Closed Jewish holidays.
Admission free.
Tours in English, Yiddish, and Hebrew.
Access: Subway: JFK airport train; E, F to Union
 Turnpike, then board the Q10 bus to airport.
 Car: Take Triborough Bridge to Grand Central
 Parkway to Van Wyck Expressway to airport.
 Enter JFK area #2. Pass public parking lots
 #2 and #4, then make a right turn at the sign
 that reads Van Wyck Expressway airport exit.
 Look for Chapels parking signs.

83

The Firefighting Museum of the Home Insurance Company

59 Maiden Lane (William Street), New York, N.Y. 10038 (212) 530-6800

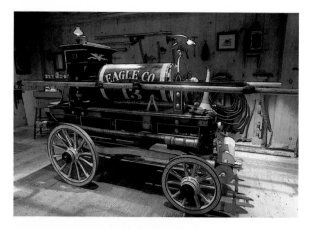

When the doors open on the fifteenth floor of the 44-story Home Insurance Company headquarters, it is more than a bit surprising to see in the middle of the room an old wooden hand-pump fire engine. This is the Firefighting Museum's introduction to what may be the most outstanding collection of nineteenth-century fire-fighting equipment in the country.

These colorful costumes, helmets, parade hats, presentation shields, hoses, trumpets, buckets, fire marks, models, toys, and other memorabilia from the old days of volunteer firemen are owned by the Home Insurance Company, and it is their intention to show the relationship between fire and insurance. However, the public relations angle is extremely subtle and in no way interferes with the intent of the three large rooms as a museum.

One of the most interesting displays shows more than 1,400 fire marks. Originated in England in the seventeenth century and first used in America in the middle of the eighteenth century, these were plaques with an insurance company's symbol given to clients who had taken out a fire policy on their homes. The fire marks were posted on the insured person's property, and they inspired volunteer squads to respond quickly—and often to argue bitterly about who had gotten to the scene first—since the insurance companies were generous with bonuses and other perks to the fire fighters.

Below the fire marks are trumpets and buckets. The buckets, made of leather, were required by law in every home, and homeowners often decorated them to match their decor. Having the most attractive fire bucket was the source of some neighborly competition.

Speaking trumpets are actually megaphones, and they were used by foremen to direct their teams. Included here is one owned by Tammany Hall's "Boss" Tweed, who was a fire marshal at one time.

A highlight of the museum is the reconstruction of the Eagle Engine Company No. 13, which in the nineteenth century was located just a few blocks from the museum on Maiden Lane. Large double doors open onto a room made from 150-year-old timber, with a James Smith hand-pump engine in its center-floor ready position. On the walls are leather hoses, buckets, ropes, axes, tools, lanterns, and other paraphernalia of a well-equipped company.

By mid-1982 museum may merge with New York City Fire Department Museum at new location. Call number above for information.

Hours: Tu-Th: 10-3:45. Closed major holidays.

Admission free.

Access: Subway: #2, 4, 5 to Fulton Street; A, E to Broadway/Nassau Street. Bus: M1, 6, 15.

Car: Parking difficult.

84

The Floating Foundation of Photography

Pier 40 South, North River (Houston and West Streets), New York, N.Y. 10014   (212) 242-3177; 431-3126

"I had never seen a purple boat, so I thought, 'Why not?'" says Maggie Sherwood, co-founder and curator of the Floating Foundation of Photography. "Purple, water, and photography ...they all go together. Each has a certain energy that feeds from one to the other."

A purple boat with photography exhibitions? Why not? Located in the Hudson River, just south of Pier 40 at Houston and West Streets, the foundation is a barge with a houseboat atop it. The purple is complemented by yellow and white touches, skylights, and boxes of flowers in season. It really is a pleasant place to visit, and the exhibits are quite unusual.

So far the 100 or so shows since 1970 have included three of UFO, Kirlian, and spirit photography, called *Phantoms of the Camera 1, 2 & 3; Not on the Menu,* old and new photographs of Chinatown; *Sidelines,* photos taken by people who have other occupations (including singer Richie Havens, choreographer Louis Falco, entertainer Cleo Laine, a fire fighter, a baker, an energy consultant, a correctional officer, and Edmondo Zacchini—the Human Cannonball, formerly with the Ringling Bros. Barnum & Bailey Circus).

One purpose of having the foundation on water is so that it can travel to those who cannot come to it. As a kind of community "happening," the barge periodically travels to small towns on the Hudson, where it conducts classes and workshops. There is also a tradition of holding extension workshops in prisons and hospitals, with exhibits emerging from that work. Bellevue, Ossining Correctional Facility, Rahway, Wards and Rikers Islands, and other institutions are among those that the foundation has visited.

Lunch and dinner are often available on the barge, and visitors are always welcome to relax on deck with a book or magazine from the library, soaking in the good energy of purple and water and photography.

Hours: Th-Su: 12:30-6.
Admission by donation.
Lectures and tours in English, French, German, and Spanish by appointment.
Access: Subway: #1 to Houston Street. Bus: M10. Car: Parking nearby.

Franklin Furnace Archive

112 Franklin Street (West Broadway), New York, N.Y. 10013   (212) 925-4671

If you have been wondering what to do with your back issues of *Soup Magazine* or that complete set of "100 Boots" postcards, take them to the Franklin Furnace Archive.

The unusual mission of Franklin Furnace is to collect, catalog, and conserve those multiple-edition, artist-produced books, magazines, pamphlets, records, cassette tapes, and other ephemera generally judged by the public to be "throw-away" items.

Although the concept of the page as art space began in 1909 with the Futurist Manifesto, it burgeoned after World War II, when photocopy, offset, and other inexpensive printing methods became widely available. In 1976 artist Martha Wilson founded the Franklin Furnace to keep examples of this form of art from becoming lost. The permanent collection of over 7,000 items includes such gems as *Paranoids Anonymous Newsletter*, in which all entries are signed with a thumbprint, and *Bikini Girl Magazine*, which prints on pink paper.

Also found in the archives is *The Art & Project Bulletin*, the publication begun in Amsterdam in 1968 that launched the popular trend of sending this kind of artwork through the mail.

Exhibits in the roughly hewn nineteenth-century loft change every three weeks. They in-

clude work by individual artists and such historical shows as *The Page as Alternative, from 1909–1980* and *Eastern European and Russian Books, 1910 to the Present*.

Every Thursday multimedia artists perform their work. These performances combine the concept of the page as art space with one or more other art forms, resulting in events that are as unique as the museum's collection.

Hours: Tu-Sa: 12-6. Closed major holidays.
Admission free.
Lectures given occasionally and by appointment.
Access: Subway: #1 to Franklin Street; #6, A, AA, CC, E, N to Canal Street. Bus: M1, 6, 10, 22. Car: Parking lot nearby.

Fraunces Tavern Museum

54 Pearl Street (Broad Street), New York, N.Y. 10004   (212) 425-1778

Fraunces Tavern Museum is one of the few Revolutionary period sites that doesn't claim to have put up George Washington for the night. It has a better drawing card—the Long Room of the tavern is where General Washington on December 4, 1783, bid an emotional farewell to his officers before leaving for Annapolis to resign.

Today, visitors to the museum brush past Wall Street bankers and brokers having lunch in the ground-floor restaurant (*not* part of the museum) and walk up one flight to the Long Room, which has been faithfully restored. The room has not been bumped upstairs to accommodate the restaurant; dining rooms in the eighteenth century were commonly located on the second floor, and this room is the original.

Across the hall from the Long Room is a charming reconstruction of a Federal-style dining room, and a third room contains memorabilia, including such prizes as one of George Washington's teeth encased in a locket and a lock of his hair, which was actually brown.

Built as a single-family home for Etienne Delancey in 1719, the building became a tavern under the ownership of Samuel Fraunces in 1762 and has been a tavern ever since. It has also been a frequent center of political activity—from meetings in 1762 of the Sons of Liberty and local merchants to protest their oppression under the English to the terrorist bombing that damaged part of the site in the mid-1970s.

The building and museum are owned and maintained by the Sons of the Revolution in the State of New York. The focus of the collection is the Revolutionary War and George Washington memorabilia, but the range of exhibits extends to life in eighteenth- and nineteenth-century America. Exhibits have included a look at tea as a social, economic, and decorative influence and a study of the Jewish community in New York from 1654 to 1790.

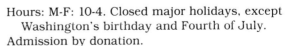

Hours: M-F: 10-4. Closed major holidays, except Washington's birthday and Fourth of July.
Admission by donation.
Tours in any language by appointment for a fee. Picture-taking without flash permitted.
Access: Subway: #4, 5 to Bowling Green; #1 to South Ferry; E, RR to Whitehall Street. Bus: M1, 6, 15 to South Ferry. Car: Garage and lot parking nearby. Metered street parking.

87

French Cultural Services

972 Fifth Avenue (79th Street), New York, N.Y. 10021   (212) 570-4400

Entering the lobby of French Cultural Services is like walking into a fairy tale. Sixteen marble columns ring the room, which is light and white with small touches of pale color. In the center, a naked cupid presides on a small fountain. The floor is inlaid with copper molding and the walls are all white marble. On one wall is a fireplace taller than a grown man. Painted on the ceiling are pale green leaves twining through a yellow-white trellis and eight medallions of playful children.

The mansion was a private home built around 1902 as a wedding gift to Helen Hay from her parents when she married Payne Whitney. The French government bought it in 1952 and uses it as the main branch of the embassy's cultural, press, and information services, apparently untroubled by the fact that this splendor was inspired not by French taste but by sixteenth- and seventeenth-century Italian design.

It is this most extraordinary setting that serves as the gallery of the French Cultural Services. Photography is the medium most often shown because, as the attache admits, "the space does not lend itself so well to other art forms." Indeed, the space would compete too much.

Six times a year photography exhibitions are mounted—photos by French photographers or, occasionally, by Americans working on a French theme. From time to time one American and one French photographer have a joint show of work that addresses a common theme. But mostly it is French photographers, both venerable and emerging.

In the past, it has been possible to see such exhibits as Lucien Aigner's photographs of Paris life around Bastille Day. Other exhibits have offered a French architect's images of New York architecture and eleventh- and twelfth-century French Romanesque murals.

Hours: M-F: 10-5. Closed major holidays.
Admission free.
Bilingual research library.
Access: Subway: #6 to 77th Street. Bus: M1, 2,
   3, 4. Car: Limited street parking or use
   Metropolitan Museum of Art parking lot.

French Institute/Alliance Française

22 East 60th Street, New York, N.Y. 10022 (212) 355-6100

FROM VINES TO WINES
Photographs by
Peter Aaron
Aug. 7 – Sept. 25

The small gallery of the French Institute/ Alliance Française may not be as thrilling as the Louvre, but it is one of New York's best substitutes for Francophiles who desire a soupçon of culture.

All of the exhibitions center on some aspect of French-speaking culture. But that could be Swiss or Belgian or Haitian, and beyond language anything goes.

You might find *Art & Biscuits,* a show about the French biscuit company Lefèvre-Utile's savvy pre-1914 advertising strategies. Creator of the "LU" biscuit, Louis Lefèvre-Utile understood the importance of promotion. He used every available ploy to increase his market—

trompe l'oeil boxes shaped like a train, a Russian roulette wheel, a canoe, or a stack of plates; posters, collector's cards, and postcards by popular artists; and, perhaps most inspired, picture postcards of actresses, painters, bishops, and explorers proclaiming the merits of "LU" biscuits with autographs, verses, or music. To quote Sarah Bernhardt: "I can't think of anything better than a 'petit LU.' Oh! yes! Two 'petits LU…'"

Or here are photographs taken by Michelle Vignes of Parisian concierges, those all-knowing superintendents of apartment buildings. Or Art Deco posters. Or picture postcards from 1889 to 1919, the Golden Age. Or photographs of tap-taps from Haiti, bold paintings on Haitian buses that are commissioned by their owners to instill confidence in patrons.

Hours: M-Th: 10-8, F: 10-5:30, Sa: 10-1:30.
  Check hours during August and September.
  Closed Christmas week.
Admission free.
Lectures in French. Picture-taking and research
  facilities by permission.
Access: Subway: #4, 5, 6 to 59th Street; RR to
  5th Avenue. Bus: M1, 2, 3, 4, 32. Car: Parking
  lot nearby.

89

The Frick Collection

1 East 70th Street, New York, N.Y. 10021   (212) 288-0700

The Frick is one of the two most peaceful spots in New York. (The other is the Cloisters.) One step into the Garden Court—with its arched glass ceiling, marble columns, plants, and fountain with bronze water-spouting frogs—and jangled nerves are soothed. Doors from the court lead into the surrounding rooms, filled with religious and secular masterpieces.

Henry Clay Frick, the Pittsburgh coke and steel industrialist, was the last individual to build a block-long mansion in Manhattan. He wanted a place to house the art he had collected over a 40-year period, and he wanted that place to be on Fifth Avenue. So when the Lenox Library on the corner of Seventieth Street was torn down, Frick bought the land, hired architect Thomas Hastings, spent $5.4 million to construct a home in the style of eighteenth-century Europe, and in 1914 moved in. It was his intention that the mansion be converted to a public museum after he and his wife died. This was done in 1935.

Only the first floor is open to the public, but that in itself is at least sixteen rooms. To retain the atmosphere of a private home, the art is eclectically arranged in the furnished rooms. Although it is difficult to conceive of such a palace as having been the scene of domestic routine, the arrangement is pleasing, largely because different rooms evoke different moods.

The Boucher Room, for example, has eight panels representing the *Arts and Sciences* painted by François Boucher for Madame de Pompadour. Needless to say, they are ornate, romantic, and very French. In comparison, the living room, with its stunningly focused *Saint Francis in Ecstasy* by Bellini on one wall and the stark *Saint Jerome* by El Greco on another, arouses quite a different set of emotions.

Masterpiece follows masterpiece: a portrait of George Washington by Gilbert Stuart, Piero della Francesca's *Saint Simon*, Jan van Eyck's *Virgin and Child, with Saints and Donor*, a self-portrait by Rembrandt.

In the mansion's calm atmosphere, even such great work is not overwhelming. Rather, it is impressive and inspiring and so pleasing to be near that when you come upon J.C. Johansen's portrait of Henry Clay Frick, which hangs in its rightful place above the fireplace in the library, you pause and quietly thank Mr. Frick.

Photograph opposite © The Frick Collection, New York

Hours: Tu-Sa: 10-6, Su: 1-6. June through
  August: W-Su. Closed major holidays.
Admission fee charged.
Wheelchairs available by advance appointment.
  No children under ten allowed. Lectures given
  October through May. Research facilities
  available by appointment.
Access: Subway: #6 to 68th Street. Bus: M1, 2,
  3, 4, 30. Car: Street parking only.

91

The Fulton Ferry Museum
The National Maritime Historical Society

2 Fulton Street, Fulton Ferry Landing (under Brooklyn Bridge), Brooklyn, N.Y. 11201   (212) 858-1348

In the shadow of the Brooklyn Bridge and next door to Brooklyn's chic River Café, a little yellow-shingled fireboat station sits on the site of a lot of history. It is that history—of the site itself, New York Harbor, and seafaring in general—that is the business of the Fulton Ferry Museum and its administrator, the National Maritime Historical Society, which operate out of the building.

Even before this spot was used as the evacuation point for General George Washington's troops from the Battle of Long Island, an enterprising farmer named Rapelje, who owned the land, would stop his field work and row *Breaukelenites* to New Amsterdam whenever someone rang the bell he had posted near the shoreline. This was ferry service à la 1642.

In 1814 Robert Fulton's *Nassau* made the runs, and by 1872 ferries were making 1,200 crossings daily. After the construction of the Brooklyn Bridge in 1883, the ferry was on its way out, although service continued until 1923.

The two-story Marine Fireboat Station No. 7 was built in 1930. In 1976, the museum and society moved there from the South Street Seaport, which is where the ferry used to dock on the Manhattan side.

In the quaint ground-floor gallery, with its tin walls and ceiling, the Fulton Ferry Museum honors the Port of New York. Exhibitions of prints, photographs, models of sailing ships, and marine artifacts alternate with spotlight shows on the contemporary community—for example, the work of artists who have taken over lofts in the area known as DUMBO, an acronym for Down Under Manhattan Bridge Overpass.

Of particular interest is the Visiting Ships Program, which allows boats to moor at the museum's pier if they remain open to the public. The Hudson River sloop *Clearwater,* the Spanish trader *Berta,* and a Chinese junk are among the vessels that have visited.

Hours: M-Su: 12-6. Check in advance for holiday hours.
Admission free.
Research facilities by appointment.
Access: Subway: #2, 3 to Clark Street; #4, 5 to Boro Hall; A to High Street. Car: From Brooklyn Bridge or Brooklyn-Queens Expressway take Cadman Plaza West exit, and follow Cadman Plaza West all the way to the river. Turn right onto Fulton Street. Limited parking nearby.

92

Galeria Venezuela
7 East 51st Street, New York, N.Y. 10022   (212) 826-1660

The drapes and carpet in the large storefront window are an unlikely tartan plaid, but the sign over the door reassuringly reads Republic of Venezuela.

Galeria Venezuela is the exhibition space of the Venezuelan consulate general, which has its offices here along with the comptroller general and the tourist bureau. The consulate purchased the building in 1973, and the gallery opened in 1976.

In six exhibitions a year of two months each, Galeria Venezuela gives exposure to the work of Venezuelan artists. All media are shown—photographs, prints, drawings, paintings, and sculptures. The work encompasses a wide variety of influences and schools: photorealism, surrealism, expressionism, pop. There is a particularly strong showing of op and kinetic art, which have enjoyed great popularity in Venezuela.

The gallery owns a small collection (about 20 pieces) of paintings, drawings, prints, and photographs that have been donated to it by artists. Sometimes these works are incorporated into group shows, but generally they are not on display.

The space is a medium-sized, one-room gallery, located on street level. Behind the main gallery space is a row of busy offices, where telephones ring and voices call out in the quick sounds of Spanish. Additional pieces of art hang here on a long wall. Plans are being made for a complete renovation so that the entire ground floor will be devoted to the gallery. The offices will be upstairs, and the exhibition space will almost double its current dimensions. A permanent display of the 20 pieces from the collection will be mounted in a large square lobby on the second floor.

Hours: M-F: 9-4. Closed major American and
    Venezuelan holidays.
Admission free.
Occasional lectures and tours in English and
    Spanish by appointment.
Access: Subway: E, F to 53rd Street/Fifth
    Avenue. Bus: M1, 2, 3, 4. Car: Parking
    inconvenient.

93

The Galleries at F.I.T./The Shirley Goodman Resource Center

Southwest corner of 27th Street and Seventh Avenue, New York, N.Y. 10001 (212) 760-7760

The Fashion Institute of Technology is ideally located, right in the middle of the section of Seventh Avenue that is home to so many designers' and wholesalers' showrooms and that has come to be known as Fashion Avenue. And so what better place could there be than the school's Shirley Goodman Resource Center to show wild, wonderful, and dramatic exhibitions about fashion from hats to boots?

The center's four galleries (one on the ground level and three on the lower level) offer a huge amount of space in great, attractive rooms that are completely redesigned for each exhibit.

There are the expected shows honoring fashion's finest designers, Paul Poiret, Galanos, and the like. But since F.I.T. as a school (it is a division of the State University of New York) offers far more than just fashion, so do the galleries. For example, an exhibition of contemporary packaging (such as perfume bottles, milk cartons, and shopping bags); the history of window display plus specially created "dream windows"; lovely snuggly quilts from the nineteenth and twentieth centuries; and children's clothing from 1790 to 1980.

A tour of F.I.T.'s extensive and extraordinary collection of costumes, textiles, and accessories—1.5 million articles of clothing and 3 million textile swatches, to be exact—should not be missed. Imagine a room the size of a city block with row upon row of gray file cabinets filled with old lace, Chinese embroidery, polished cotton. (Each piece, of course, is meticulously cataloged.) Then imagine on top of the file cabinets rows of hats, fans, parasols, shoes, handbags, and other accessories, many donated by such celebrities as Joan Crawford and Lauren Bacall.

Then, if you are not already overwhelmed, imagine another room, also a city block long, with racks and racks of clothes labeled Chanel, Dior, Norell, and so on. From Balenciaga to blue jeans, from beaded gowns to bikinis, fashion past and present is documented. The tour is by advance appointment.

Hours: Tu: 10-8, W-Sa: 10-5. Closed legal holidays.

Admission free.

Lectures and tours by appointment for a fee. Picture-taking by permission.

Access: Subway: #1 to 28th Street; AA, CC to 23rd Street. Bus: M10, 16, 26. Car: Parking lots nearby.

94

The Garibaldi-Meucci Museum

420 Tompkins Avenue (Chestnut Avenue), Staten Island, N.Y. 10301   (212) 987-1926

Poor Antonio Meucci. Fate, it seems, was never kind to him, even after his death. Take, for example, the very home where he lived, a simple white clapboard house in the Rosebank section of Staten Island. His name stands second on that landmark, now a museum, because Meucci was kind enough to take in Italian war hero Giuseppe Garibaldi for 18 months. Not only that, but it appears that Garibaldi remains an imposing houseguest. The museum's exhibits are overwhelmingly dedicated to him.

Born in 1807, Giuseppe Garibaldi was a ball of fire, a fighting man who had a rather rocky relationship with the Italian government. As a young man he joined up with Giuseppe Mazzini, chief of the Italian nationalists and revolutionaries in the 1830s. After he was discovered plotting a revolution, Garibaldi fled to South America, where he was involved in several other revolutions. During this exile, from 1836 to 1848, he founded the Redshirts, an Italian legion that specialized in guerrilla warfare.

In 1848 he returned to Italy, but he was exiled to America after failing to defend Rome against a French attack. It was then that he moved into Antonio Meucci's Staten Island home, where they eked out a living by hunting and making candles for sale.

Garibaldi returned to Italy in 1854, participated in more campaigns, became a hero for his role in the liberation of the south of Italy, had more disagreements with the government, and eventually retired to the island of Caprera, where he died in 1882.

Antonio Meucci, born in 1808, came to America in 1845 and settled on Staten Island. He produced a working model of a telephone in 1857, obtaining a patent for it in 1871, five years before Alexander Graham Bell and Elisha Grey presented their inventions to the patent office within an hour of each other. But the patent office had lost Meucci's papers, and consequently he had to forfeit all rights to the invention. By the time the Supreme Court in 1886 declared Meucci the first inventor of the telephone, it was too late for him to benefit and he died in 1889 a bitter, poverty-stricken man.

The museum-house praises Garibaldi in purple prose, and along with photographs, letters, medals, and documents, it displays such items as his red shirts and locks of hair. The corner devoted to Meucci includes his death mask and wooden models of his telephone. In the backyard is a giant concrete caldron where these two unlikely comrades made candles out of wax.

Hours: Tu-F: 10-5, Sa & Su: 1-5.
Admission free.
Tours by appointment.
Access: Subway to Ferry: #1 to South Ferry: #4, 5 to Bowling Green; N, RR to Whitehall Street. Bus to Ferry: M1, 6, 15. After Ferry: Bus: #103. Car: Turn left onto Bay Street, then right onto Vanderbilt Avenue. At first light turn left onto Tompkins Avenue. Parking nearby.

95

Goethe House New York—German Cultural Center

1014 Fifth Avenue (82nd and 83rd Streets), New York, N.Y. 10028 (212) 744-8310

Rare work photos, stills, scripts, and other memorabilia from the making of the 1925 silent film *The Joyless Street*, starring Greta Garbo. The disturbing construction collages of Nuremberg-born Ilse Getz, with their dolls' heads, cutouts of parrots, eggs, medieval damsels, and cigarette butts. Searing caricatures from *Simplicissimus*, the satiric weekly begun in Munich in 1896. Novelist Herman Hesse's life—witnessed through photographs, his own drawings, poems, and book jackets. Nineteenth-century drawings of an airship, a bicycle, a submarine, a glider, from the Deutsches Museum in Munich.

These have been the subject of shows at Goethe House New York, the city's German cultural center, where throughout the year exhibitions are mounted on aspects of Deutschland's arts and sciences. And along with them is a full roster of films, lectures, readings, and concerts and a library of 16,000 German and English books.

In this distinguished Beaux Arts townhouse located directly across from the Metropolitan Museum of Art, exhibits start in the lobby and continue up the elegant winding staircase into a room with decorative moldings and a fireplace.

Some years a specific theme is chosen and followed throughout the programming. In the late 1970s it was *Berlin Now*, which drew record crowds. In 1981 *Germany in the 19th Century* was highlighted, with subjects ranging from the life of Sigmund Freud to *Art and Architecture between Classicism and Romanticism*.

Hours: Tu & Th: 11-7, W, F & Sa: 12-5. Closed
   Fourth of July through Labor Day.
Admission free.
Limited wheelchair access.
Access: Subway: #4, 5, 6 to 86th Street. Bus:
   M1, 2, 3, 4. Car: Use Metropolitan Museum
   parking lot. Street parking difficult.

96

The Governor's Room at City Hall

City Hall (Warren and Broadway), New York, N.Y. 10007   (212) 566-5525

City Hall, with its combination Louis XIV–Federal design, is a surprisingly elegant base of operations for a city that has the reputation of having an often less-than-gracious citizenry. Be that as it may, City Hall is the seat of New York City's government, and both its architecture and art collection are worthwhile sights.

The most important pieces of city-owned art are in the Governor's Room on the gallery level. When you first enter City Hall the lobby leads into a superb coffer-domed rotunda, which extends the full height of the building and has a double-curved stairway leading directly to the door of the Governor's Room. The rotunda and gallery are so impressive that they have been used for important civic ceremonies. Here, at the head of the stairway in front of the Governor's Room, Abraham Lincoln lay in state on April 24 and 25, 1865, while lines of mourners extended down the stairs and into the streets.

The Governor's Room was used from 1814 to the 1920s as an office for New York's governors on their visits to the city. Today, the long central room and smaller east and west chambers display historical portraits by John Trumbull, furniture made for City Hall upon its completion, and some earlier furniture taken from Federal Hall.

The most notable piece is the desk used by George Washington from April 1789 to August 1790, when Federal Hall served as the first capitol. A Trumbull portrait of Washington hangs over the west fireplace mantel. On the opposite wall is a portrait of George Clinton, the state's first governor. These and the ten other Trumbull portraits that hang in the room were commissioned by the Common Council to glorify the new nation's leaders.

Busts and portraits of mayors, governors, and various other government officials can be found throughout the halls and chambers, which for the most part are open to the public. Together, the pieces present not only a history of the state's leaders but a lesson in American portraiture.

Hours: M-F: 10-4. Closed major legal holidays. Admission free.

Picture-taking with flash or tripod by permit only.

Access: Subway: #4, 5, 6 to Worth Street; E to World Trade Center. Bus: M1, 6. Car: Garage parking nearby.

97

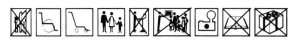

Grey Art Gallery and Study Center

New York University, 33 Washington Place at Washington Square East, New York, N.Y. 10003   (212) 598-7603

The Grey Art Gallery and Study Center is one of those clean, well-lighted places that makes looking at art a pleasure. Manageably sized yet spacious enough to mount substantial exhibitions, the Grey Art Gallery aims at innovative and diverse programming. In fact, it seems to have the kinds of exhibits you didn't realize were missing from your life until the Grey reminded —and satisfied—you. These are not "blockbuster" shows; rather, the themes are slightly off-beat. For example, watercolors, drawings, and books by that marvelous Victorian Beatrix Potter, the originator of Peter Rabbit and other heart-warming characters. Or the most extraordinary photographs from the first decade of *Life*.

The gallery's permanent collection of 4,000 pieces concentrates on late-nineteenth- and twentieth-century works, with a particular strength in American paintings from the 1940s through the present. Exhibitions run from six to eight weeks, and approximately five exhibitions are mounted each year, including one from the permanent collection.

The gallery's innovative attitude toward exhibitions is not surprising considering its history and location. Operating as New York University's (N.Y.U.) fine arts museum, the Grey Art Gallery and Study Center is located in an open loft-type space on Washington Square Park in Greenwich Village, a center of cultural life for years. The gallery itself occupies the site of the first academic fine arts department in America, established in 1835 by Samuel F. B. Morse. From 1927 to 1942 the space housed A. E. Gallatin's Gallery of Living Art, one of two public spaces in the city to show nonrepresentational art at the time.

Unfortunately, N.Y.U. was not interested in maintaining Gallatin's collection, and so he moved it to the Philadelphia Museum of Art. By 1958 the university had revised its attitude and founded the N.Y.U. Art Collection, but it wasn't until 1975 that the Grey Art Gallery was opened with a gift from Mrs. Abby Weed Grey.

Hours: Tu & Th: 10-6:30, W: 10-8:30, F: 10-5, Sa: 1-5. June through August: M-F: 1-7. Closed major holidays and Christmas through New Year's Day.

Admission free.

Lectures, tours, and research facilities by appointment. Picture-taking by permission.

Access: Subway: #6 to Astor Place; B, D, E, F to West 4th Street; N, RR to 8th Street. Bus: M1, 2, 3, 5, 6. Car: Parking nearby.

98

The Grolier Club

47 East 60th Street, New York, N.Y. 10022   (212) 838-6690

In the foyer of the Grolier Club is an 1890 painting that depicts the printer Aldus showing bindings to the French bibliophile Jean Grolier. Inaccurate in nearly every detail, the painting is simply a nineteenth-century illusion of sixteenth-century printing. To have this canvas hanging in the home of a club dedicated to the book arts is an indication of the wit and self-assurance of the Grolier Club.

Founded in New York in 1884, the club was formed to promote awareness and interest in the traditional arts of the book—design, paper, printing, illustration, and binding. Today its membership, which is scattered around the world, includes 655 rare book, manuscript and print collectors, curators, librarians, and dealers.

In keeping with the tradition of the club, a main activity of members today is the planning of free exhibitions that demonstrate the best of the past and the present in book arts and literature. The exhibition season runs from October to June, with four major shows lasting six weeks each. The themes of the exhibits always center around books, manuscripts, and illustrations.

For example, in celebration of James Joyce's birthday the club held a showing of a complete collection of first editions of his prose and poetry, plus original photographs and letters to and from Joyce.

Exhibits often extend beyond books and papers and into the realm of memorabilia. A show on Gertrude Stein included a photograph of Stein wearing a vest and next to the photo the vest itself. A tribute to John Donne included his signet ring.

The clubhouse, erected in 1916, is a handsome building designed by a member, Bertram Grosvenor Goodhue. The exhibition hall, which takes up most of the ground floor, is a large open room, two stories high. On the second story is a balcony lined with books. Glancing up at it as you wander through the ground floor displays serves as a reminder that this place is a book lover's haven.

Hours: During exhibitions: M-F: 10-5, Sa: 10-3.
 Other times by appointment. Closed major
 holidays.
Admission free.
Access: Subway: #4, 5, 6, N, RR to 59th Street.
 Bus: M1, 2, 3, 4. Car: Garage parking nearby.

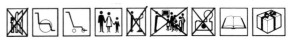

Guinness World Records Exhibit Hall

Empire State Building, 34th Street and Fifth Avenue, New York, N.Y. 10118 (212) 947-2335

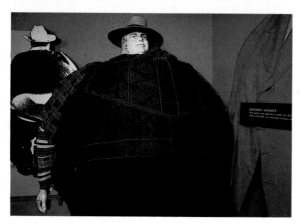

The Empire State Building makes most people think "up," but those who take the escalator down to the concourse will enter the Guinness World Records Exhibit Hall—a tribute to extraordinary occurrences of nature and human tenacity. Displays of more than 200 recordbreakers taken from *The Guinness Book of World Records*—the largest, the smallest, the highest, the fattest, the most—vie for attention.

Perhaps to pay homage to the 102-story building in which the hall is housed, the first exhibit a visitor sees on entering is a statue of the tallest man who ever lived, Robert Wadlow, who measured 8 feet, 11.1 inches. The Empire State Building itself was the entry for the tallest building until 1972, when it lost to the World Trade Towers, which in turn lost its place to the Sears Tower in Chicago.

This is the place to learn who holds records for the greatest number of consecutive situps, pushups, and jumping jacks. Video monitors placed throughout the hall show many of the recordbreakers performing their feats. You can also see a photograph of the oldest living thing, the Bristlecone Pine, which is 4,600 years old and can be found on the California side of the White Mountains. Followers of the smallest will discover that the tiniest orchid is found in Australia; it has flowers that measure less than 0.04 inch.

And movie fans can see Katherine Hepburn's three Oscars on display. Hepburn holds the record for the most Academy Awards won for the category of starring role, although in sheer numbers she is widely displaced by Walt Disney, who picked up 35 Oscars during his career.

Family-minded visitors will enjoy learning about the largest and smallest babies, the oldest bride and bridegroom, the longest engagement, and the largest puppy litter.

And for those skeptics who must split hairs, yes, there is Englishman Alfred West's—a single strand neatly divided into fourteen parts.

Hours: Daily: 9:30-6:30. Closed Christmas and New Year's Day.

Admission fee charged. Children under six free.

Access: Subway: #6, B, D, N, QB, RR to 34th Street. Bus: M2, 3, 4, 5, 16. Car: Parking lots nearby.

The Hall of Fame for Great Americans

Bronx Community College, University Avenue & West 181st Street, Bronx, N.Y. 10453. (212) 220-6187

The view alone is reason enough to visit the Hall of Fame for Great Americans—a vista stretching over high rises and train tracks, across the Harlem River to a picture-postcard panorama of the Cloisters in Fort Tryon Park and beyond to the Palisades. This is the highest natural point in the City of New York, located on the former University Heights campus of New York University, now Bronx Community College.

The Hall of Fame is a majestic 630-foot-long outdoor colonnade founded by N.Y.U. in 1900 and designed by Stanford White to honor historically significant American men and women. Built in a sweeping semicircular Neo-Classical arc with wings at either end, it is a unique and patriotic reminder that this country's phenomenal growth has been due to the vitality, ingenuity, and intellect of these individuals.

Ninety-eight bronze busts are set along both sides of the arcade, each with dates and a quote. The path begins with Elias Howe, who patented the first sewing machine, and Alexander Graham Bell, credited with inventing the telephone. The careers of these two men add an interesting counterpoint to the melody of the American way: Howe's invention, although first to be patented, was commercially outranked by Isaac M. Singer's, thus making his name more famous. As for Bell, it is disputable whether he was the true originator of the phone, even though he has received total credit.

Represented are inventors (Robert Fulton, George Westinghouse, the Wright Brothers), statesmen (William Penn, Patrick Henry, Woodrow Wilson), jurists (Oliver Wendell Holmes, Jr., John Marshall), soldiers (Ulysses S. Grant, Stonewall Jackson), educators and reformers (Susan B. Anthony, Booker T. Washington), authors (Walt Whitman, Harriet Beecher Stowe, Edgar Allan Poe, Washington Irving), and artists from various disciplines (John James Audubon, James Abbott McNeill Whistler, Edwin Booth).

Three buildings—Gould Memorial Library, flanked by the Language and Philosophy Halls—also built by Stanford White sit between the Hall of Fame and the campus. Gould Library was designed to resemble the Parthenon. The panels on its bronze doors were created by eight of Stanford White's friends and dedicated to his memory in 1921.

Hours: M-Su: 10-5.
Admission free.
Access: Subway: #4 to Burnside Avenue. Car: Take FDR Drive north to Major Deegan Expressway to West 179th Street exit, then follow signs for Bronx Community College. Parking on premises.

The Harbor Defense Museum

Fort Hamilton (101st Street and Fort Hamilton Parkway), Brooklyn, N.Y. 11252   (212) 630-4349

The city of New York's only military museum is located on the only active Army post in all of the boroughs. To get to the Harbor Defense Museum, you enter Fort Hamilton and proceed directly to the Caponier, a beautifully renovated flank battery now used to house a fine collection of cannons, guns, mines, and other objects.

New York Harbor, a primary thoroughfare for trade and the main impetus to the development of New York, has also been vulnerable to attack, a fact proved by historical events.

On July 4, 1776, simultaneous with the signing of the Declaration of Independence, a small American battery on the site of present-day Fort Hamilton fired into H.M.S. *Asia*—an act of symbolic opposition to the British. By August the Battle of Long Island, the Revolutionary War's largest battle, had started at the site.

New Yorkers became even more sensitive to the importance of harbor defense, especially during the War of 1812. As a result the construction of Fort Hamilton, named for the first secretary of the treasury, began in 1825.

About half of the original fort remains, including the Caponier. Used to protect the fort against land attack, the Caponier is probably the nation's earliest example and the best ex-

tant specimen of its kind.

The first display to the left of the entrance holds a steel helmet, sword, and chest armor from the sixteenth century. Beyond are uniforms, banners, cannons (including one from the original armament), guns, and other military equipment. There is a shiny brass Gatling gun, which was the first effective machine gun, even though it needed to be hand cranked and required four men to operate. Another item of interest is a "torpedo" mine, the kind that inspired Admiral Farragut to proclaim "Damn the torpedoes, full speed ahead."

Hours: M, Th & F: 1-4, Sa: 10-5, Su: 1-5. Closed holidays, except Memorial Day, Fourth of July, and Veteran's Day, and for a ten-day period over Christmas and New Year's.
Admission free.
Lectures and tours by advance appointment.
Access: Subway: RR to 95th Street/4th Avenue. Car: Take Brooklyn Bridge to Brooklyn-Queens Expressway east to Belt Parkway east to Fort Hamilton/4th Avenue exit. Take 4th Avenue, then turn right onto Marine Avenue, then right onto Fort Hamilton Parkway to the end.

102

Henry Street Settlement, Louis Abrons Arts for Living Center

466 Grand Street (Pitt Street), New York, N.Y. 10002   (212) 598-0400

The Henry Street Settlement has been dispensing comfort and serious doses of aid to residents of the Lower East Side since it was established at the turn of the century. And though some of its buildings are as old as a sweatshop, the arts complex is an exception. The Louis Abrons Arts for Living Center, built in 1974, is a shiny glass and brick structure, with steps forming an attractive amphitheater. At the top of the steps there is an arc of windows, behind which are the art exhibitions, a theater, and rooms for classes and workshops in the performing and visual arts.

Approximately seven times a year new shows are mounted, exhibits that are diverse except for their philosophical commitment to aiding the careers of emerging, minority, and women artists. "Exchanges" shows, in which the art has been selected by other artists, are an example of that commitment.

The types of exhibitions you will encounter here are best described by such past shows as *Regalia*, which featured the most farfetched clothing—a gown made of plastic garbage bags, a cloak made of men's ties, a peignoir with steel-wool lapels, a bracelet of dice, a shirt from used airmail envelopes; or a retrospective of the work of 80-year-old Joseph Delaney, a black American scene artist whose theme is parades, from the Easter parade to the welcome home for the hostages in Iran; or *Homework*, which recorded women artists' reactions to the domestic landscape; and *Gargoyles and Cherubs*, an exhibition of color photographs of the Lower East Side taken by Ed Fausty and Brian Rose. Once each year the work of the settlement's faculty, artists-in-residence, and students is displayed.

If you are not already in the neighborhood, the settlement is a bit of an eastward trek. Head for the Williamsburg Bridge and you can't miss it—the building's architecture is a surprise, especially those windows. What's behind them will pull you in.

Hours: M-Sa: 12-6. Closed major holidays.
Admission free.
Picture-taking by permission.
Access: Subway: F to Delancey Street; J, M to Essex Street. Bus: M14, 15, 22. Car: Street and lot parking nearby.

103

The Hispanic Society of America

155th Street and Broadway, New York, N.Y. 10032 (212) 926-2234

Bottom photograph courtesy of the Hispanic Society of America

Hours: Tu-Sa: 10-4:30, Su: 1-4. Closed major holidays.

Admission free.

Record and slides about the museum available in English and Spanish. Picture-taking without tripod permitted. Research facilities available to scholars. Scholarly publications produced by the society available.

Access: Subway: #1 to 157th Street/Broadway; AA to 155th Street. Bus: M4, 5. Car: Street parking nearby.

Enter Spain—the tears of Mary for her Son, the dark eyes of a pretty little girl, the clicking of castanets and heels at a fiesta. Enter Spain—by walking through the doors of the Hispanic Society and into a Renaissance-style courtyard of carved terra cotta, surprisingly, beautifully red.

But before that surprise there is another: the museum's setting. And behind both is a rather incredible man.

Archer Milton Huntington, the son of a railroad magnate, became fascinated with Spain and its culture when he was a teenager. With extraordinary zeal and intelligence, Huntington dedicated his life to the pursuit of Spanish culture. He learned Arabic as well as Spanish, traveled extensively, and sponsored excavations. In 1908 he opened the Hispanic Society's museum and library in a grand bit of architecture built specifically for this purpose.

What you see first is an impressive plaza with imposing limestone buildings on either side. Halfway down on the right is a sunken terrace with a huge sculpture of El Cid, done by Huntington's wife, Anna Hyatt Huntington. Directly across from El Cid is the museum.

Inside you will discover religious paintings and portraits by Goya, El Greco, Velázquez; chests and cabinets inlaid and intricately carved; decorated tiles and lustreware plates; the sixteenth-century tomb of the Duchess of Alburquerque; fabulous silverwork and bronze doorknockers and Roman artifacts.

To the left of the thirteenth-century *Mater Dolorosa* ("Sorrowful Mother")—carved out of a single piece of wood—is a particularly interesting portrait by Goya of the Duchess of Alba, dressed in black as a *maja,* a beautiful girl of the people. On her right hand are two rings inscribed ALBA and GOYA; her index finger points to the ground, where the date 1797 is traced upside down for her to read. When the painting was cleaned in 1959, it turned out that something else had been written where she points: together with Goya's signature appeared the word SOLO, the inscription thus reading SOLO GOYA ("no one but Goya"), leading to obvious speculation on their relationship.

Another highlight in this museum are the 14 murals by Joaquín Sorolla y Bastida of scenes from the provinces of Spain. Commissioned by Huntington in 1911, they depict in beautiful color and movement such festivals, festivities, and work situations as the opening salute at a bullfight in Seville and men hauling fish from a wharf in Ayamonte.

The Institute for Architecture and Urban Studies

8 West 40th Street, New York, N.Y. 10018   (212) 398-9474

Photograph courtesy of the Institute for Architecture and Urban Studies

Among the buildings constructed each year a few structures go up that are outstanding for the integrity and innovation of their design. These are buildings that make you want to know more —about how they were built and about the architects (nameless to the general public, except in rare cases) who were responsible for that design.

It is these buildings and these master builders who are recognized in the exhibitions at the Institute for Architecture and Urban Studies. The institute, which is the center in this country for theoretical architecture, likes to organize exhibits that combine the theoretical with a concern for built work. It also likes to be the first in the field to explore new issues. Hence it was here that the show that investigated and drew up proposals for low-rise housing in high-density neighborhoods as an architectural alternative was mounted.

Dedicated as well to fostering international exchange, the institute has introduced the work of Japanese, Austrian, Argentinian, and, for that matter, Californian architects who are not yet known in our part of the world. For these shows the architects are usually invited to lecture and tour the country.

Then there are the retrospectives, such as one recent tribute to Raymond Hood, the architect responsible for the RCA Tower at Rockefeller Center, the Daily News Building, the American Standard Building (located a few doors from the institute), and the old McGraw-Hill Building in New York.

Once you've studied the cleanly rendered architectural drawings and models at this remarkable institute, you'll inevitably find yourself approaching the city with a whole new frame of reference.

Hours: M-F: 9-5. Closed major holidays.
Admission free.
Picture-taking by permission.
Access: Subway: #1, 2, 3, 4, 5, 6, A, E, N, QB,
    RR to 42nd Street. Bus: M1, 2, 3, 4. Car:
    Garage parking nearby.

105

The Interchurch Center

475 Riverside Drive (120th Street), New York, N.Y. 10115   (212) 870-2932

On a square plot of land two blocks south of the General Grant National Memorial on Riverside Drive stands the 19-story Alabama limestone high rise known as the Interchurch Center. Religious groups, like all institutions, have business to conduct, and providing space for such business is the main function of the center, which rents offices to Protestant, Orthodox, and Jewish organizations on 18 of its 19 floors. On the ground floor are an interdenominational chapel, lobbies, and three small exhibition rooms.

The Orthodox Room features the most interesting exhibit. Here you'll find a display of Byzantine ecclesiastical art of the Eastern Orthodox Church. The room itself is richly decorated with floral designs painted on the ceiling and archway in blues, golds, purples, and greens. Thirteen glass cases hold icons (from the Greek word meaning "image"), sacred altar vessels, gospels, vestments, and illuminated manuscripts.

A parchment manuscript from the year 1200 is the oldest artifact in the room. Except for its antiquity, it pales next to the brilliant icons with their enamelwork frames, halos encrusted with stones, and robes made all of pearls. A display case in the archway has an authentic architectural model of a Byzantine church done in gold.

106

Across the lobby are the two other exhibition rooms. The Treasure Room has exhibits that change every month, and the tiny adjoining RSV Bible Room displays the final manuscript copy of the Revised Standard Version of the Bible and Apocrypha.

Hours: M-F: 9-4:30. Closed holidays.
Admission free.
Wheelchairs accommodated through Claremont Avenue entrance. Picture-taking by permission.
Access: Subway: #1 to 116th Street. Bus: M4, 5, 104. Car: Street parking nearby.

International Center of Photography

1130 Fifth Avenue (94th Street), New York, N.Y. 10028   (212) 860-1777

If asked what might be in the red-brick Federal–Georgian townhouse on the corner of Ninety-fourth Street and Fifth Avenue, a reasonable guess would be Duncan Phyfe sofas and Gilbert Stuart portraits. With its absolutely symmetrical, box-shaped façade, it looks like that kind of building. In fact, nothing could be further from the truth. No teapots and silver bowls here, but "images of man that are both works of art and moments in history." Put less poetically: photographs.

The International Center of Photography is the city's first and only museum devoted exclusively to this medium. Through regularly changing exhibits, the classics of nineteenth- and twentieth-century photography can be seen, work that might have been lost if Cornell Capa, its founder and director, had not worked passionately to establish the place.

The passion, unfortunately, stems from tragedy. Capa was for many years a photographer for *Life.* The photographs of his brother, Robert, were even better known. In 1954, when Robert was killed by stepping on a land mine in Indochina and, at that same time, Werner Bischof, a close friend and colleague, died in an automobile crash in Peru, Cornell Capa became haunted by the question of what would become of the work of these men and other photojournalists.

It took twenty years (and the impetus of another death—that of photographer David "Chim" Seymour in 1956) for the International Center of Photography to open. But today it is the foremost institution of its kind, with exhibitions, publications, labs, classes, and a collection of about 5,000 prints, hand cameras, films, and tapes.

The exhibitions are the sort that will move you. They are the kinds of photographs we all loved in *Life,* they are Cartier-Bresson and Atget and Arbus and Stieglitz and Weston…they are the documentation of our lives.

Hours: Tu: 11-8, W-Su: 11-5. Closed major holidays.
Admission fee charged, except Tuesdays, 5-8.
Picture-taking and library facilities by appointment.
Access: Subway: #6 to 96th Street. Bus: M1, 2, 3, 4. Car: Street and garage parking nearby.

Jacques Marchais Center of Tibetan Art

338 Lighthouse Avenue (Richmond Road), Staten Island, N.Y. 10306   (212) 987-3478

It would seem most unlikely that an attractive stone house on a quiet residential street in the middle of Staten Island would contain the largest private collection of Tibetan art in the Western Hemisphere. Nevertheless, here it is, the Jacques Marchais Center of Tibetan Art.

The museum is a single high-ceilinged stone room designed to resemble a Tibetan monastery. Throughout the room and on the three-tiered silvery stone altar, are bronze images, paintings, ritual artifacts, and instruments not only from Tibet but also from Japan, Nepal, China, India, and Southeast Asia.

Some are sensuous, graceful images of male and female deities reaching out with numerous arms or seeing 360 degrees by virtue of heads on every side. These symbolize mercy, compassion, infinite wisdom. Others are terrible and fearsome figures who act as protectors of the dharma (the teachings of Buddha).

One group of images to become acquainted with are Shinje, helpers of Yama, the Judge of the Dead. When you die, Shinje visit and take your soul to Yama so he can decide where you will be placed on the wheel of life and under what section you will be reborn.

Outside the museum is a lovely terraced garden with a lotus pond, a view of the Lower Bay, stone animals, and a Buddha of Infinite Light.

You may well wonder who this gentleman named Jacques Marchais is. In fact, he was a she, an American actress who took the name for the stage. When she married her third husband, a wealthy businessman, Marchais was able to realize her lifelong interest in Tibetan art.

Jacques Marchais was not a convert to Buddhism, and she never visited Tibet. But she was quoted as having said, "I simply worship beauty—sometimes I think I am a pagan." Be that as it may, she had a terrific eye for Eastern art.

Hours: April through November: Sa & Su: 1-5; June through August: F, Sa & Su: 1-5. All other times by appointment.

Admission fee charged. Research facilities by appointment.

Access: Subway to Ferry: #1 to South Ferry; #4, 5 to Bowling Green; N, RR to Whitehall Street. Bus to Ferry: M1, 6, 15. After Ferry: Staten Island Rapid Transit Train: To Newdorp, then take a taxi. Bus: #113 to Lighthouse Avenue and walk up hill. Car: Turn left onto Bay Street, then right onto Vanderbilt Avenue, which becomes Richmond Road. Go about 15 minutes on Richmond Road to Lighthouse Avenue, and turn right.

Japan House Gallery

333 East 47th Street, New York, N.Y. 10017   (212) 832-1155

There is a feeling that washes over you when you enter the lobby of Japan House. It is a serenity that emanates from the decor itself—the low, slatted ceiling, the shallow pond with bamboo trees, the recessed lighting. It is a fitting headquarters for the Japan Society, an association founded in 1907 to bring the peoples of Japan and the United States closer.

The Japan House Gallery, located on the second floor, is another lovely space. It is a well-proportioned, open room that is completely renovated and altered for each of the four exhibitions mounted annually. These are some of the most exciting exhibits in New York.

Borrowing from the great public and private collections (including the emperor of Japan's), the gallery shares with American audiences the breadth and diversity of Japanese art, from the earliest openwork metal temple decorations to the most recent videotapes.

Some shows are quite lavish; for example, the 63 priceless objects from Japan's premier Buddhist temple, the Hōryū-ji, founded in 607.

There also are the expected exhibits of painted screens, exquisite ceramics, colorful scrolls, richly embroidered textiles, and finely crafted lacquer. But Japanese art extends beyond these kinds of pieces and so does the scope of the gallery. You might also find Japanese music scores, ranging from the oldest manuscript in the world (a 1472 collection of Buddhist chants of the Shingon sect) to the most contemporary and innovative notations combining Eastern and Western traditions. Or a fog machine that is controlled by an artist to make ephemeral sculptures in the air. Or photographs of Japanese life from 1854 to 1905. Or superb eighteenth- and nineteenth-century drawings. All of it is exotic and enchanting.

Hours: Daily: 11-5, F: 11-7:30 during exhibitions.
Admission by donation.
Occasional lectures on exhibitions. Tours and research facilities by appointment.
Access: Subway: #4, 5 to 42nd Street; #6 to 53rd Street. Bus: M15, 27, 101. Car: Parking lots nearby.

The Jewish Museum

1109 Fifth Avenue (92nd Street), New York, N.Y. 10028   (212) 860-1888

Wherever Jewish people have lived—and in 4,000 years' time that is almost everywhere—they have affected and been affected by the culture of the host country. With this in mind, the Jewish Museum is truly an international museum, emphasizing the cultural and artistic rather than the religious life of Jews throughout the world.

When an exhibition on a particular festival or tradition is mounted, examples from many cultures are shown. For example, an exhibit on marriage contracts will have framed pieces from Persia, Istanbul, and Italy. A display of goblets will feature those from France, Spain, and Poland.

The beautifully carved wood wainscoting of the former Felix M. Warburg mansion, which houses the museum, serves as a backdrop for the Torahs, spice boxes, Sabbath candlesticks, Menorahs, and other ceremonial objects in the museum's extensive collection of Judaica.

Its collection of fine arts includes work by Jewish artists and work by non-Jews on Jewish themes. One prized piece is a Rembrandt portrait of a Jewish bride. The earliest coin can be found in the display of coins and metals.

Administered by the Jewish Theological Sem-

inary of America, this is the kind of museum people come to when they need expert advice. The research staff for the movie *Raiders of the Lost Ark* came to study the Biblical themes of illustrator James Jacques Joseph Tissot when they were working on the film. (An exact replica of the ark as depicted by Tissot shows up as a book illustration in the movie.)

The museum has a varied schedule of educational programs: everything from Sephardic music concerts to lectures on Kafka to how to make archaeological tools. The Tobe Pascher Workshop produces contemporary ceremonial objects.

Hours: Su: 11-6, M-Th: 12-5. Closed F, Sa, certain legal holidays, and major Jewish holidays. Call museum for details.

Admission fee charged. Members free. Senior citizens by donation.

Wheelchairs available. Twice a month certain programs will be signed to the hearing impaired. Picture-taking without flash permitted.

Access: Subway: #4, 5, 6 to 86th Street. Bus: M1, 2, 3, 4. Car: Sylvan's Garage between Park and Madison Avenues gives a slight discount with a museum-validated ticket.

111

J. M. Mossman Collection of Locks

20 West 44th Street, New York, N.Y. 10036   (212) 840-1840

Locks. They keep people out and they keep people in. They are probably the most peaceful and legal form of protection. Certainly, the General Society of Mechanics and Tradesmen of the City of New York has excellent locks on its doors, for that is where the J.M. Mossman Collection of Locks is located. As for J.M. Mossman, he was a member of the society who lived from 1850 to 1912. The society itself was started in 1785 and has continued since then without interruption.

The society's headquarters is a grand, staid, old building with lots of carved wood, marble, and brass. On the ground floor is a good-sized library that is open to the public. A marble staircase leads you to the second-floor balcony, which holds the J.M. Mossman Collection in wonderful wooden cases that haven't been tampered with in years.

Case after case is filled with familiar and mysterious locks, all seemingly in mint condition with mechanisms showing. There are antique keys and wooden locks and locks with such extraordinary names as Chinese padlocks and Egyptian, Magic, and Double Quadruplex key locks. One large piece of machinery that looks like it would defy any crook is simply labeled "A Very Complicated Lock." There is a shiny brass prison lock and there are combination, double combination, and combination trick locks. All in all there are 400 locks, mostly dating from 1850 to 1912.

Although names and catalog numbers are given for the locks, the labeling fails to answer the kinds of questions such a display naturally inspires. More detailed information is given in a book titled *The Lure of the Lock,* a 246-page hardcover book that, in addition to providing the key (so to speak) for each lock, includes essays on such topics as ancient locks, skeleton keys, secret locks, and lock picking. It is a rather fascinating volume that can be borrowed as an aid for viewing the collection or purchased at a nominal price.

Hours: M-F: 10-4. Closed during July and major holidays.

Admission free. Picture-taking by permission only.

Access: Subway: #1, 2, 3, 7, A, AA, B, CC, D, E, F to 42nd Street. Bus: M1, 2, 3, 4, 5, 6, 7, 10, 32. Car: Parking lots nearby.

112

Just Above Midtown/Downtown

178-80 Franklin Street (Hudson Street), New York, N.Y. 10013 (212) 966-7020

The tile work above the door reads "Roethlisberger & Co. Established 1856." But unless Roethlisberger is an alternative art space also known as Just Above Midtown/Downtown, then that company must now be established somewhere else.

"This was a meat-packing plant," says Linda Goode Bryant, JAM/D's founder and director. "In 1980 when we moved in, it was one big refrigerator in here." It was after the move, from Fifty-seventh Street to this once-chilly, now-comfortable Tribeca gallery, that Just Above Midtown added Downtown to its name.

In the 1960s, while a history of figurative art by blacks was being uncovered and new work was being exhibited, particularly that with political themes, abstract art was being given no credence. Bryant started JAM/D in 1974 when, after working at the Metropolitan Museum of Art and the Studio Museum in Harlem, she realized that there was no place for Afro-Americans to showcase abstract art.

Over the years JAM/D's focus has broadened to include the work of black, white, and Third World artists, making it an unusual space if only for that reason. Taking a cue from the emerging neighborhood—the Tribeca warehouse district, which is quickly going the way of Soho, with a chic restaurant here, a line of renovated lofts there—JAM/D shows the work of emerging artists in two thematic and eight solo or two-person shows each year.

One fascinating show, called *Crossovers,* featured the art of creative people who are primarily known for work in another medium. Lighting up the walls for that exhibit were such stars as Diane Keaton, Kurt Vonnegut, Candice Bergen, David Bowie, Martin Mull, Ornette Coleman, and Joni Mitchell.

A second gallery, in the basement, called "Undercurrents" acts as a lab where artists can test work in progress. There are also programs: Friday night films, publications, and seminars on the business of being an artist. One recent program involved various kinds of artists (visual, dancers, performers, musicians) working publicly at JAM/D for a three-week period and then exhibiting or performing what they created.

Photographs courtesy of Just Above Midtown/Downtown

Hours: During exhibitions: Tu-Sa: 11-6. Closed August and major holidays. Call before visiting.
Admission free.
Lectures and tours by advance appointment.
Access: Subway: #1 to Franklin Street; #2, 3 to Chambers Street; A, AA, CC, E, N, RR to Canal Street. Bus: M1, 6, 8, 10, 22. Car: Limited parking nearby.

113

The Kingsland House

143-35 37th Avenue (Parsons Boulevard), Flushing, N.Y. 11354   (212) 939-0647

Within sight of its neighbor the Bowne House is a Dutch and English farmhouse known as the Kingsland House, a yellow structure with a gambrel roof built in 1774. It is a sturdy place, having survived such traumas as the Revolutionary War, fire, vandalism, and relocation. You see, you couldn't always glimpse Kingsland House from the Bowne's backyard.

Originally, Kingsland House was located in a spot that was slated to become a shopping center in 1968. Concerned citizens went to work to save the historic house, moving it to Weeping Beech Park.

The Kingsland House was kept in one family for nearly 100 years. Built by Charles and Sarah Doughty, the home went to their daughter Mary and her husband, Joseph King, and then to their daughter Mary Ann and her spouse, Lindley Murray (after whose family the Murray Hill section of Manhattan was named).

Currently, the house is used as headquarters for the Queens Historical Society. Rather than compete with the Bowne House's fine original furnishings, the society has chosen to use the space for exhibits. In this way the two houses serve as companions.

The parlor and dining room are used for exhibitions that change about every four months —from quilts to old Christmas picture postcards

to costumes from the 1860s to 1930s. The corridor/pantry, which connects the rooms, is used to display china and clothing from the Murray era.

On the second floor is the library of the Queens Historical Society and a Victorian period room. A large closet in the hall holds a display of enticing objects that Aunt Mary Murray, a spinster who lived in the house, collected for her nieces and nephews. Aunt Mary's closet has buttons and silk purses and early paper dolls and enough other small items to delight any child.

Kingsland House is shaded by a tree that has its own landmark status—an enormous weeping beech. It was planted in 1847 by Bowne descendant Samuel Parsons, a nurseryman who brought the shoot from a baron's gardens in Belgium. All other weeping beeches in this country, it is said, come from this old tree.

Hours: Tu, Sa & Su: 2:30-4:30. Closed Christmas and New Year's Day.

Admission by donation.

Picture-taking by permission.

Access: Subway: #7 to Main Street. Car: Take Triborough Bridge to Grand Central Parkway. Exit at Northern Boulevard, then turn right onto Parsons Boulevard. Go one block and make a left onto 37th Avenue. Street parking nearby.

The Kitchen

484 Broome Street (Wooster Street), New York, N.Y. 10012   (212) 925-3615

When the Kitchen picked its name in 1971, it was a decision to opt for the literal. The old Broadway Central Hotel between Mercer Street and Broadway had been converted into the Mercer Arts Center, and some people began showing videotapes in what had been the hotel kitchen. The name stuck, even when, in 1974, the Kitchen moved farther downtown to an unfashionable warehouse district called Soho.

From the outset, the Kitchen was experimental (video was an avant-garde form that no one else was showing in 1971) and it remains so today. Over the years music, dance, and performance have been added, though not like anything you have seen or heard before. For example, what started as conceptual art has gradually moved toward conceptual performance, and just as the art did not resemble Rembrandt, the performances are nothing like Chekhov.

As video has become increasingly sophisticated, so has programming at the Kitchen. In its second-floor Soho loft in a massive and magnificent corner building, the Kitchen each year invites hundreds of artists to cook up some unusual recipes.

The first room you enter is the gallery where ten video and multimedia installations are mounted annually. The emphasis here is on creating a sculptural or environmental atmo-sphere with video and other elements. It is quite different from the regular screenings, which are more like watching TV. Images differ vastly according to each artist's vision; for example, you might see eight monitors showing the sunrise burning across Paris rooftops or you might listen to electronic music as abstract images slowly melt into one another. What you will *not* see at the Kitchen are framed canvases.

In the viewing room, a small comfortable space with gray-carpeted banquettes, five hours of videotapes are showcased daily. The large main loft space is used for a regularly changing program of screenings and performances.

Public access to experimental performance and video is being increased by the Kitchen's touring program, which takes artists and tapes as far as the Soviet Union. Public spaces around New York are also being infiltrated by Kitchen-supported projects. Look for video screens in store windows, bus terminals, and airports.

Hours: M-Sa: 1-6. Closed July and August.
Admission free to gallery and video room.
Limited wheelchair access. Occasional night
  lectures.
Access: Subway: #1, A, AA, CC, E to Canal
  Street. Bus: M6. Car: Garage parking nearby.   **115**

Korean Cultural Service Gallery

460 Park Avenue (57th Street), New York, N.Y. 10022 (212) 759-9550

Sense of Serenity, the title of a recent exhibition, is the feeling conveyed by the Korean Cultural Service Gallery, where the contemporary and the traditional combine to make a most pleasing whole.

The gallery itself is a soothing room with slate gray carpeting, pale gray Haitian cotton walls, and groupings of low upholstered chairs. Seven to eight times each year this room is the setting for an introduction to a facet of Korea's rich cultural identity. You might see:

You Hyun-Ju: The palest, most delicate shades of rose, green, violet, tangerine, and aquamarine embroidered on gauzelike blinds called ramie fabrics. Some of the designs are uniform geometrics, and others are lovely abstract landscapes.

Minhwa: The art of fantasy and dreams as interpreted through folk paintings that reveal an uncomplicated and romantic world of happiness and humor.

Kugak: The traditional music of Korea, played with flutes, zithers, lutes, clappers, drums, and gongs for court, military, and religious ceremonies and, of course, for sheer pleasure. Stunning costumes complement the instruments for occasions such as the Nightingale Dance or the Ball Throwing Dance.

The gallery also steps firmly into present-day art by exhibiting the work of contemporary Korean painters. Artists and performers are frequently brought in for lectures and performances in the gallery. The Korean Cultural Service also co-sponsors major exhibitions at New York museums—*5,000 Years of Korean Art,* at the Metropolitan Museum of Art, and drawings by contemporary artists, shown at the Brooklyn Museum, were two recent shows.

The gallery is located on the sixth floor of an office building called the Korea Center. It and its umbrella, the Korean Cultural Service, are a branch of the consulate general of the Republic of Korea.

116

Hours: M-F: 9-6. Closed major holidays.
Admission free.
Occasional lectures and tours in English and Korean. Picture-taking by permission.
Access: Subway: #4, 5, 6 to 59th Street. Bus: M1, 2, 3, 4, 15, 101, 102. Car: Parking lots nearby.

Lefferts Homestead

Prospect Park (Empire Boulevard/Flatbush Avenue), Brooklyn, N.Y. 11215   (212) 965-6511

The front of Lefferts Homestead faces busy Flatbush Avenue. The back looks out on the Children's Farm of Prospect Park Zoo. What, might you ask, is a Dutch farmhouse built around the time of the Revolution doing here? The answer is that this structure was not the original house owned by the Lefferts family, and neither was it originally on this site. Nevertheless, the house and its story are authentic and provide yet another link to the history of New York City.

Construction on the handsome two-story wooden structure, which was the home of Lieutenant Peter Lefferts, began in 1777. The new house would replace Lefferts's great-grandfather's home, which was burned in the Battle of Long Island in August 1776 by Washington's troops because the British were occupying it. The new home, built with some lumber, nails, and hardware salvaged from the original home, remained in the Lefferts family and was used as a dwelling until 1918. It then was given to the City of New York, which moved it from Flatbush Avenue between Maple and Midwood Streets to the current site at the Prospect Park Zoo.

The place badly needs fresh paint and general maintenance work. Also the furnishings have not been arranged realistically to simulate life in a Colonial farmhouse. But the structure itself is one of the last remaining Dutch Colonial farmhouses in Brooklyn.

Front and back porches, Dutch-style front doors, and a dramatic gambrel roof provide a gracious façade to the house. The interior consists of a hall that goes straight through from front to back doors, with two rooms on either side. The second floor has the same layout.

A detail to note is the plaster centerpiece in the parlor ceiling, a scallop pattern of 16 stars. If the stars are interpreted to represent the number of states at the time, the work was done between 1796 when Tennessee became the sixteenth state and 1803 when Ohio joined the Union.

All the rooms have furnishings from the mid-1700s to the mid-1800s, including some pieces from the Lefferts family (the grandfather clock in the parlor). Unfortunately, the rooms are cordoned off at the doorjamb with iron gates, and so it is difficult to get a sense of the space. Still, it is interesting to see sleigh and canopy beds, cradles, bed warmers, spinning wheels, a quilting frame, a meat grinder, and other artifacts from this time in history, including the coffeepot owned by Enoch Hale, brother of Nathan "Give me liberty or give me death" Hale.

Hours: Daily: 1-4:30. Closed every second Saturday of each month November through May.
Admission free.
Access: Subway: D, M, QB, S to Prospect Park. Car: Take Manhattan Bridge to Flatbush Avenue, then turn right onto Empire Boulevard. Street parking nearby.

117

Library & Museum of the Performing Arts
The New York Public Library

111 Amsterdam Avenue (64th Street), New York, N.Y. 10023   (212) 870-1630

To stop time and capture for one split second the magic of a ballet or Broadway musical, to see close up how that magic was created, to understand more clearly the life and work of a great talent—this is what is possible at the Library & Museum of the Performing Arts at Lincoln Center. Three galleries and several alcove and wall spaces are the setting for wide-ranging displays on theater, dance, and music.

There are two entrances to this comfortably modern building, which is wedged between the Vivian Beaumont Theater and the Metropolitan Opera House. One is on Lincoln Center Plaza, where three glass display cases suspended on a wall greet you. The other is on Amsterdam Avenue. If you use that entrance, the Amsterdam Gallery is directly to your right. The other two large exhibition spaces, the Main Gallery and the Vincent Astor Gallery, are on the second floor.

Exhibits frequently cover the life and work of an individual: the opera singer Richard Tucker, who was also a cantor; Zero Mostel, who was a serious oil painter in addition to being a successful actor; Nijinsky, the spellbinding dancer who began drawing after he went mad. Exhibits include all aspects of the person's life. In the case of Nijinsky, there were extraordinary photographs, a sculpture by Auguste Rodin that was inspired by Nijinsky, drawings by Jean Cocteau, and the dancer's own mad drawings.

Another kind of show consists of drawings and models of costumes and stage sets; for example, those of Boris Aronson, the designer for such hits as *Company, Follies, Fiddler on the Roof, A Little Night Music,* and *The Diary of Anne Frank.* This kind of exhibit is fascinating because once we have seen the show the costumes and sets remain in our memory. It is a wonderful opportunity, then, to study them closely and to remember how they enhanced the performance.

Hours: M & Th: 10-8, Tu: 10-6, W, F & Sa: 12-6. Closed major holidays.
Admission free.
Wheelchairs accommodated via Lincoln Center Plaza entrance. Tours and lectures by appointment. Picture-taking by permission.
Access: Subway: #1 to 66th Street; A, AA, B, CC, D to 59th Street. Bus: M5, 7, 10, 11, 29, 30, 104. Car: Garage parking on premises for a fee. Limited street parking.

118

The Long Island Historical Society

128 Pierrepont Street (Clinton Street), Brooklyn, N.Y. 11201   (212) 624-0890

In a terra-cotta building in Brooklyn Heights are nineteenth-century paintings, prints, photographs, documents, maps, coins, firearms, flags, and banners that have remained untouched for over 80 years and are only now being rediscovered.

Brooklyn in the mid-nineteenth century was a center for abolitionists and extremists. It was their belief and great fear that the Civil War signaled the end of the world. This concern coupled with the fact that the area's population was doubling each year inspired a group to create the Long Island Historical Society in 1883 to capture the area's vanishing past.

The collection process was rapid, and by 1887 the grand home of the society was being built by George W. Post. But by 1900 the founders had all died, and although the society managed to remain open, the library of 125,000 books and the collections of art and artifacts collected dust. Only in the last few years has the great wealth begun to be cataloged and restored.

Greeting visitors as they enter the building is a seated cigar-store Indian wearing a feathered headdress and smoking a pipe. On the foyer's walls and up the stairs that lead to the library are portraits of historical luminaries and important personages from Brooklyn society.

The library is in itself an artifact that should not be missed. A beautiful room, two tiers high, carved in black ash with stained glass windows on the second tier and large light-filled windows on the first, it looks and feels in every way like the dream of an old library. It even smells of books and bindings.

Work continues upstairs to clean and catalog more art and artifacts. A huge room on the fourth floor is spilling over with photos and banners and cannonballs and heaven knows what else. By 1983 that room is scheduled to open to the public as a display and study center.

Hours: Tu-Sa: 9-5. July: M-F: 9-5. Closed August and major holidays.
Admission free.
Research facilities available for a fee.
Access: Subway: #2, 3, 4, 5 to Clark Street or Boro Hall. Car: Take Brooklyn Bridge to Cadman Plaza West exit. Turn left onto Cadman Plaza West, then right onto Montague Street, then right onto Clinton Street; next street is Pierrepont. Parking difficult.

119

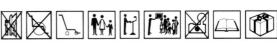

Manhattan Laboratory Museum

314 West 54th Street, New York, N.Y. 10019   (212) 765-5904

Who am I? Who are all these people around me? Where and how do I fit into the rest of the world? These are questions many of us silently ask ourselves all our lives. But children, who are not yet intimidated, actively express such puzzlements. An adult may well wonder where to take children to help them figure these things out. *Answer:* To the Manhattan Laboratory Museum, where cultural anthropology, perception, and the natural sciences are translated into simple participatory exhibits that are fun for both kids and adults.

Where else can you turn lights on and off just by walking up and down a flight of stairs? Or use your voice to make a laser beam dance? Or "freeze" your shadow against a phosphorescent screen? Or see a shoebox city that undergoes urban expansion whenever someone adds a building, and where the "architects" have given their structures names such as Wendy's Place or Made by Brenda of Borough Park, Brooklyn?

In another part of the multilevel room are masks—some to look at, some to try on—and materials (washable paints, wigs, and hats) for making your own from that natural mask, the face. And in yet another area of the museum is a living model of the Central Park lake, stocked with bullfrogs, turtles, guppies, toads, and newts. Two anole lizards, Samson and Delilah, are in a nearby cage, and aquariums are filled with crabs, catfish, a lobster, and other underwater creatures indigenous to the Northeast coast. A cage of live crickets (food for Samson and Delilah) cause a racket reminiscent of the country.

The museum calls itself a laboratory because it is always experimenting with the best presentations of nature, culture, and art that children can utilize to better understand their world and to expand their horizons. Founded in 1979 and housed in a renovated courthouse, it operates under the auspices of G.A.M.E. (Growth through Art and Museum Experience), an organization that develops creative approaches to learning through the arts and humanities.

A full schedule of programs is constantly in motion, from making clay "animalitas" to devising games with paper bags. In the basement where the exhibits are built, the public is invited to participate in workshops or to visit the casting room where students have been working on a life-sized dinosaur skeleton.

Hours: Tu-Sa: 11-5.
Admission fee charged, except Thursdays.
Groups of ten or more by appointment. Museum store specializes in high-quality science- and art-related projects.
Access: Subway: AA, CC, B, D, E to 59th Street. Bus: M10, 27, 104. Car: Parking nearby.

120

Marine Museum of the Seamen's Church Institute

15 State Street, New York, N.Y. 10004   (212) 269-2710

From New York Harbor or even closer from Battery Park, you can see a most unusual feature on one of Manhattan's southernmost buildings: a gigantic cross the height of the 24-story brick building of which it is a part. Facing the harbor, the cross serves as a sign of welcome for the crews of the 7,300 ships that dock every year in the Port of New York and New Jersey. They know that the building is the Seamen's Church Institute of New York and New Jersey, which has been serving seafarers of all nations since 1834 with ecumenical comfort, aid, and special programs.

The Marine Museum of the Seamen's Church Institute has an excellent collection of ship models, marine prints, paintings, and nautical artifacts on permanent display throughout its five floors. The public is invited to wander freely through the corridors, discovering cases filled with rare treasures.

The institute owns over 300 ship models, about 100 of which are on display. Perhaps the most fascinating group is about 75 small international boats—from Chinese junks to South Sea outrigger canoes—that have been donated by heads of state (including Winston Churchill, Madame Chiang Kai-shek, and Emperor Hirohito). Outstanding among these models is the decorated Royal Boat of the King of Siam.

Nineteenth- and twentieth-century paintings and prints by such noted marine artists as Gordon Grant, Frank Vining Smith, Frederick Cozzens, Antonio Jacobsen, and Charles Robert Patterson depict a variety of nautical scenes, from calm harbors to ships being thrashed about in storms. There are the intricate knots of macrame (originally a sailor's art that was adopted by landbound craftspeople) and on the fourth floor a unique display of tattoo designs.

In the Visitors' Center on the street level, four to five exhibits are mounted each year. Drawn from the institute's collection and supplemented by other nautical collections, the thematic shows range from ship models and prints of seventeenth- and eighteenth-century fighting sailboats to photographs of present-day merchant vessels.

Hours: Visitors' Center: Daily: 10-3; closed major holidays. Permanent collection: M-F: 8-6.
Admission free.
Research facilities available by appointment.
Access: Subway: #1 to South Ferry; #4, 5 to Bowling Green; RR to Whitehall Street. Bus: M1, 6 to South Ferry. Car: Garage parking nearby.

121

Struggle of the Two Natures in Man
George Grey Barnard (1863-1938)
Marble, 1894
Gift of Alfred Corning Clark, 1896 (96.11)

The Metropolitan Museum of Art

Fifth Avenue at 82nd Street, New York, N.Y. 10028   (212) 879-5500

To begin by stating that the Metropolitan is one of the world's great museums is both obvious and inevitable. A day spent in these rooms and halls is a world tour, a trip in a time machine, and a thorough stretch of the "cultural" muscles.

From your first glance at the monumental façade—Roman arches and Corinthian columns, neo-Classical and contemporary wings, standing unobstructed on the edge of Central Park—you know that you will be entering a palace dedicated to the arts. The lobby, grand and always filled with fresh flowers, maintains this impression. From this point on, however, common experience ends, and the journey becomes personal.

It simply is not possible to see the entire museum in a single visit or even in several. Best to pick a few highlights or a particular wing and concentrate on that.

There are always several temporary exhibitions in progress at any one time. Frequently, there is an absolute blockbuster, such as *Treasures of Tutankhamun* or *The Splendors of Dresden* or the exhibit of over 300 masterpieces from the Vatican due in 1983.

As for permanent displays of art, there is Islamic, Greek, Roman, Eastern, European, twentieth century, Medieval, and more, as hall leads into hall. Great favorites have always been the arms and armor, period rooms, and costumes. The Egyptian Collection is world renowned and so extensive it is organized by dynasty.

New wings seem to sprout at the Metropolitan like appendages on a fantastic beast. In 1978 it was the Temple of Dendur, built by Emperor Augustus around 15 B.C. during the Roman occupation of Egypt and Lower Nubia and reassembled in a great glass enclosure (the Sackler Wing) with a spacious simulation of the entire site.

The American Wing, a great expansion of the 1924 original, was introduced in 1980. From a

Hours: Tu: 10-8:45, W-Sa: 10-4:45, Su: 11-4:45. Closed Thanksgiving, Christmas, and New Year's Day.

Admission by donation.

Recorded tours only for rent. Gallery talks in English, Spanish, and French. Picture-taking without flash permitted; tripod by permission. Research facilities available to qualified researchers and graduate students.

Access: Subway: #4, 5, 6 to 86th Street. Bus: M1, 2, 3, 4. Car: Parking on premises.

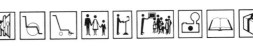

main court flanked by the Greek Revival façade of the United States Branch Bank and the floral stained glass of the garden entrance to Louis Comfort Tiffany's Oyster Bay home, the American Wing embraces every aspect of American art, from earthenware pots to John Singer Sargent's portrait of Madame X to windows by Frank Lloyd Wright.

The Astor Garden Court and the Douglas Dillon Galleries for Chinese Painting were opened in 1981. The Court, a graceful, meditative spot, is a garden of gray terra-cotta modeled on a courtyard in the Garden of the Master of the Fishing Nets in the City of Soochow. When filled with people its effect is lost, but when empty it is a special experience.

The newest wing, the Michael C. Rockefeller Collection of Art of Africa, Oceania, and the Americas, is the largest display of its kind in the world.

Midtown Y Gallery

344 East 14th Street, New York, N.Y. 10003   (212) 674-7200

The sound that leads you up the stairs of the Emanu-El Midtown YM–YWHA to the second-floor landing and through the long hallway gallery is the echo of basketballs and voices bouncing off the floors and walls. This is not an auditory illusion. The gallery ends at the Y's gymnasium. But it is a long walk to that end, and before it has ended there are worlds to visit—the worlds captured in photographs.

Since 1971 the Midtown Y Gallery has exhibited photographs, often of New York life: the city during World War II, Jewish life in the city, city games from softball to boccie to chess. Or photographs taken by New Yorkers—winners of Creative Artists Public Service Program fellowships, women photographers, photographers who have not shown before. Sometimes themes hover very close to home—*14th Street, River to River*, which looked at life on the Y's own strip.

To New Yorkers it's all thrillingly familiar: the musicians in Washington Square Park; a lone elderly man sitting on a park bench; five women chatting at the O.K. Harris Gallery, their backs to the art on the walls; the cube sculpture at Astor Place. Even bygone days seem close—sailors and War Bonds signs and the smoke-puffing Camel cigarettes billboard at Times Square.

Nine or ten times a year the world changes in the second-floor gallery. Downstairs in another hallway, a more lasting world exists. It is here that work from the permanent collection is displayed, that of Berenice Abbott, Jacob Riis, and others.

Hours: Su-Th: 12-8, F: 12-4. Closed Jewish and
    major holidays and certain summer days.
Admission free.
Occasional lectures. Picture-taking by
    permission.
Access: Subway: #4, 5, 6, N, RR to 14th Street;
    LL to First Avenue. Bus: M14, 15. Car:
    Metered street parking and lot parking
    nearby.

The Morris-Jumel Mansion

West 160th Street and Edgecombe Avenue, New York, N.Y. 10032 (212) 923-8008

Even in New York, a city of surprises, the Morris-Jumel Mansion and its immediate neighborhood are an astonishing sight to encounter. Never would you guess when you step out of the subway at 163rd Street and Amsterdam Avenue, an area that has seen better days, that just around the corner is an oasis out of the past.

The Morris-Jumel Mansion, which in 1765 rested on 130 acres and today is on one and a half, is unique in the grandeur of its scale. No prim Federal styling here, but instead a wide, columned place in the English Palladian fashion of the Georgian period.

The house was built for Colonel and Mrs. Roger Morris as a summer retreat from their townhouse near Bowling Green. With the outbreak of the Revolution, Loyalist Morris went to England, and his wife and children to her family's estate in Westchester.

General Washington chose the house as his headquarters from September 14 to October 18, 1776, because its high site offered views of both rivers. (Incidentally, Washington had at an earlier time courted Mrs. Morris, the former Mary Philipse.) Here he planned the successful Battle of Haarlem Heights and from the pillared portico on September 28 watched a large portion of the city destroyed by fire.

The house then served as British and Hessian headquarters and after that became Calumet Hall, a tavern that was the first stop on the Albany Post Road.

By 1810 it was in grave disrepair, but the mansion was purchased and restored by Stephen Jumel, a wealthy French wine merchant, and his wife, Eliza. Eliza had been a prostitute and Jumel's mistress and was the illegitimate daughter of a Rhode Island prostitute. Although beautiful (red hair and violet eyes) and not uneducated, Eliza to her distress was never accepted by New York society. (She taught herself to read and write both English and French, and sometimes passed herself off as the daughter of aristocratic French parents who had been lost at sea.)

In 1832 Jumel died of injuries from a carriage accident, and the next year Eliza married Aaron Burr—he for her money, she for his connections. The marriage lasted six months, the divorce becoming final on the day he died. Eliza died in 1865, at the age of 91.

Three periods are covered in the decor of the house—Federal, Colonial, and Empire. Because different periods are not mixed within rooms, each room retains a distinctive spirit. Eliza's

bedroom is in Empire, with much of the furniture having been acquired from Napoleon Bonaparte's family. Aaron Burr's bedroom includes his office desk, a portrait, and a traveling trunk carved from a tree. (Yes, that is how the word "trunk" was coined.)

Across the street on the west side is Sylvan Terrace, a mews of beautifully restored wooden rowhouses built in 1882. Next to Sylvan Terrace are limestone townhouses, which also have been nicely renovated. These, with their parent, the Morris-Jumel Mansion, make this site—the highest in Manhattan—one of the great undiscovered neighborhoods.

Hours: Tu-Su: 10-4. Closed Thanksgiving, December 25, and Jan. 1.

Admission fee charged.

Wheelchair and stroller access limited to first floor. Tours, lectures, and research by appointment. Guide sheet available in English, French, German, Italian, Japanese, Spanish, and Swedish.

Access: Subway: #1 to 157th Street/Broadway; AA to St. Nicholas/163rd Street. Bus: M2, 3. Car: Street parking nearby.

129

El Museo del Barrio

1230 Fifth Avenue (104th and 105th Streets), New York, N.Y. 10029   (212) 831-7272

When you enter, a young man smiles a welcome, enthusiastically hands out catalogs, and calls after you, "Just ask me any questions if you have them." El Museo del Barrio—the Museum of the Neighborhood—has retained the warmth of community through twelve years of development.

Founded in 1969 by a group of Puerto Rican parents living in East Harlem who wanted to introduce their children to Puerto Rican heritage and culture, the museum has, over the years, expanded to include all Spanish-speaking peoples, although the Puerto Rican community remains central.

Five to six exhibits are mounted each year in the whitewashed ground-floor galleries. Whether it is the intense paintings of Carlos Raquel Rivera or the sweetly poetic images of Villarini, the fascinating *autorretratos* ("self-portraits") of 29 photographers or photos of Puerto Rican civilian and political life, each exhibit instructs as well as entertains.

The permanent collection, of farm and household implements, folk art, paintings and sculptures, and works on paper, is on display in the main gallery. Also found here are the *Santos de Palo*, hand-carved and painted figures of the saints made for altars set up in the home. Photographs can be seen at the "F-Stop" gallery and a new wing is presently under construction, which will house a collection of 200 pre-Columbian objects.

The museum's programs include *Musica de Camara* ("chamber music"), folk music, and films. An annex to the museum is a recently rehabilitated firehouse on East 104th Street. It is shared with an affiliated theater group, Teatro 4, and used by El Museo as a fine arts school.

Hours: Tu-F: 10:30-4:30, Sa & Su: 11-4. Closed major holidays.
Admission free.
Wheelchair entrance on 104th Street. Lectures and tours in English and Spanish.
Access: Subway: #6 to 103rd Street. Bus: M1, 2, 3, 4. Car: Metered street parking and lot parking nearby.

130

Museum of American Folk Art

49 West 53rd Street, New York, N.Y. 10019 (212) 581-2474, 254-8296

Since 1961 the Museum of American Folk Art has been presenting the kind of exhibitions that make you proud to be an American. Not that the four shows mounted each year have hard-hitting patriotic themes. Rather, the pieces themselves—wonderfully crafted examples of folk art—underscore a strong, diverse, and inspired cultural heritage.

The Americans who made quilts and hooked rugs, weathervanes and whirligigs, carousel horses and cigar store Indians would likely be amazed to see their handiwork displayed in a museum. Yet, in today's world, where synthetic, machine-made items are the most common, the fine stitching on an Amish quilt in the Double Wedding Ring pattern or the functional whimsy of a pig-shaped weathervane is appreciated as a cultural document and as art.

The museum's permanent collection, acquired through gifts and purchases, is too extensive to exhibit in the two cozy second-floor galleries. Instead, portions of it are displayed in the quarterly exhibits, which are supplemented by borrowed works.

Sometimes exhibitions have a genre theme—hooked rugs or Amish quilts from the midwest or painted and decorated furniture. Other times themes are an image or motif—hearts or childhood or the all-American dog.

The museum owns some unusual pieces, such as a nine-foot weathervane of St. Tammany (mythical chief of the Delaware Indians), a whirligig (wind toy) of Uncle Sam riding a bicycle, Father Time with a beard of real hair and the ability to strike a bell. Then there are haughty chalkware cats and straightforward, naive-style portraits and stoneware plates for serious eating. And it is quite moving to study a Canadian goose decoy crafted by someone named Joe Lincoln and imagine this man patiently carving and smoothing and painting for practical reasons as well as for pleasure.

Hours: Tu: 10:30-8, W-Su: 10:30-5:30.

Admission fee charged, except Tuesdays, 5:30-8. Children under twelve free.

Picture-taking without flash or tripod by permission. Research facilities available by advance appointment.

Access: Subway: D, E, F to 53rd Street. Bus: M1, 2, 3, 4, 5, 6, 7. Car: Parking across the street.

131

Museum of Archaeology at Staten Island

631 Howard Avenue (Clove Road), Staten Island, N.Y. 10301   (212) 273-3300

On the third floor of the Main Hall of Staten Island's Wagner College are two atticlike rooms filled with objects from ancient and non-Western cultures. What you may see here, far from their original homes, are eight-sided Sumerian clay tablets, an Egyptian offering bearer, a bronze tripod of three bulls from sixth-century B.C. Iran, or a pre-Columbian terra-cotta figure of a seated priest, among 1,500 additional artifacts.

The museum's collections have been organized geographically, covering Egypt, the Near East, the Far East, Greece, Italy, Europe, the Americas, Africa, and Oceania. Unfortunately, the small space does not allow display of all the objects at once, and so they are brought out area by area through a series of semiannual thematic exhibitions mounted in one of the two rooms.

For example, *Divine Images & Other Fabulous Creatures* woke from hibernation such monsters as a winged, human-headed bull demon from Iran and feline and fish demons battling on a Peruvian vessel. These were joined by more sanguine images of people and animals from all over the ancient world.

The museum's other room is devoted to *New York City's Indian Heritage*, a developing, per-

132

manent exhibition that begins with the burial customs of New York Indians.

There are sections on Indian technology, domestic life, and subsistence, with displays of such objects as beaded moccasins, pipes, a necklace made from eagle claws, and carbonized food remains.

At this point the exhibit rather abruptly ends, and cases are filled with artifacts from Meso-America, Peru, the Near East, and Egypt, including a bust of the Egyptian lion-headed goddess Sekhmat.

Hours: M-Th: 10-4:30, Su: 1-4:30. Closed August and Christmas through New Year's Day.
Admission free.
Limited stroller access. Lectures, tours, and research facilities by appointment.
Access: Subway to Ferry: #1 to South Ferry; #4, 5 to Bowling Green; N, RR to Whitehall Street. Bus to Ferry: M1, 6, 15. After Ferry: Bus: #7 to Clove Road/Howard Street, then transfer to 6S Bus. Car: Turn left onto Bay Street, then right onto Victory Boulevard, then left onto Clove Road, then left onto Howard Avenue. Go up hill to Wagner College Main Building, which houses museum. Free parking on premises.

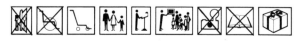

The Museum of Broadcasting

1 East 53rd Street, New York, N.Y. 10022   (212) 752-4690, 752-7684

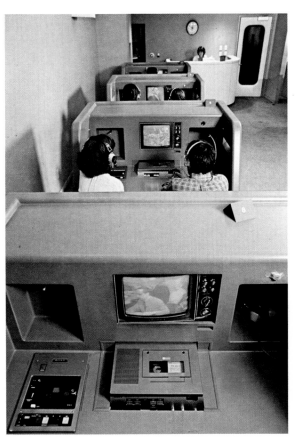

The Museum of Broadcasting must be the only museum where each visitor picks the exact exhibition he or she wants to see from a computer-generated card catalogue. In this ultramodern, somewhat futuristic environment, the subject is television and radio, and the public is invited to watch on consoles, each equipped with three sets of earphones, samples of almost any program ever broadcast.

The museum is a bountiful playground for media lovers, although selecting an hour's worth of listening or viewing from the more than 4,200 radio broadcasts dating back to 1924 and the more than 5,400 television broadcasts from 1949 to the present can be difficult. And there's more: Available on microfiche are 1,600 rare radio production scripts with handwritten alterations and timings.

This unusual museum, founded by William S. Paley in 1976, is the first of its kind in America. It is a popular spot with those who know about it; the 23 consoles and two theaters are in constant use.

On a recent visit, two teenagers were giggling so loudly over an episode of *Laugh-In* that the attendant had to ask them to be quiet. Two younger girls were as hypnotized by the Beatles on *The Ed Sullivan Show* as the fans were in 1964. A man in his thirties was watching an early version of *Amos 'n' Andy* while a businessman studied the Kennedy-Nixon debates, which according to the attendant are quite popular with middle-aged men.

Certainly there is something for everyone. Most of the early television shows are represented in the archives, and new shows are added regularly. Radio broadcasts range from Orson Welles's *The War of the Worlds* to Franklin D. Roosevelt's 1932 campaign speeches.

And for those who desire a whopping dose of commercial interruption (for reasons we won't bother to question), it is possible to arrange for the dubious pleasure of an hour's worth of advertisements.

Hours: Tu-Sa: 12-5, Th: 5:30-8. Closed Fourth of
   July, Thanksgiving, and Christmas.
Admission by donation.
Lecture series on broadcasting arts given in evenings for a fee.
Access: Subway: E, F to 5th Avenue. Bus: M1, 2, 3, 4. Car: Garage parking nearby.

Museum of Bronx History/Valentine-Varian House

3266 Bainbridge Avenue (208th Street), Bronx, N.Y. 10467 (212) 881-8900

The Bronx County Historical Society is fortunate enough to have its headquarters in a lovely farmhouse built in 1758 by a blacksmith named Isaac Valentine. Previous occupants have included Hessian, American, and British troops during the Revolution, and in later, more peaceful times Isaac Varian, the mayor of New York from 1839 to 1841, whose father bought the place from the Valentine family in 1791.

Today the grounds of the fieldstone house are well preserved with pleasant gardens and a good-sized lawn. The interior no longer resembles that of earlier days, except for the wide floorboards with their rough nails. Smooth white walls and glass cabinets and cases now serve as display areas for the Museum of Bronx History, which is run by the Bronx County Historical Society.

Permanently displayed are artifacts from Indian, settler, and Revolutionary days, including a Jew's harp and a sewing kit with needles. In another room are artifacts from more recent times: 1923 box seats from Yankee Stadium and empty bottles and wooden taps from the breweries that used to be in the area. The May 10, 1935, issue of the *Bronx Home News* advertises women's arch shoes for $1.87 a pair and

large apartments for 35 dollars a month. Of course, those being Depression days, higher prices would not have brought many takers.

Temporary exhibits on the walls of the hallway and giftshop change on an irregular basis but vary from local art to old postcards.

Downstairs is the society's fascinating research library of Bronx history, which includes 1,200 volumes (including directories from the days before telephones); 1,500 slides; 1,000 postcards; 7,000 photographs; and tons of clippings, pamphlets, maps, and ephemera. All are maintained in professional library style, making this an excellent place for digging up interesting facts about life in the Bronx.

Hours: Sa: 10-4, Su: 1-5. Closed Christmas and New Year's Day.

Admission fee charged.

Picture-taking by permission. Library available by appointment.

Access: Subway: #4 to Mosholu Parkway; D to 205th Street/Bainbridge Avenue. Car: Take FDR Drive north to Major Deegan Expressway to Cross Bronx Expressway to Bronx River Parkway north. Exit at Gunhill Road. Turn left onto Bainbridge Avenue, then left onto 208th Street. Parking nearby.

134

Museum of Holography

11 Mercer Street (Canal Street), New York, N.Y. 10013   (212) 925-0526

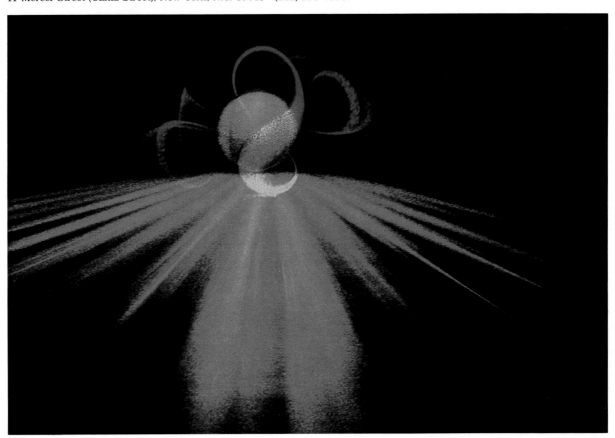

In a section of the downtown warehouse district that hasn't yet been transformed into luxury lofts and chic boutiques, nestled between Empire Sporting Goods and Freiman Coated Fabric, there sits a magical world called the Museum of Holography.

For the uninitiated, holography is three-dimensional photography produced by laser beams. The technique was discovered in 1947 by Dr. Dennis Gabor, who received the Nobel Prize in Physics for his invention in 1971. The result of Dr. Gabor's pioneering, as seen in the attractive museum, is a blending of science and art that is both fascinating and spooky.

A pretty, brown-haired woman floats behind a cage of Plexiglas. You expect her to step out any moment. But as if that surprise isn't enough, the woman blows you a kiss when you move your position slightly, making it even more difficult to accept that she is only an illusion. Throughout the museum, there exists this sensation of people and images imprisoned in a time warp, waiting to be freed.

The museum's surreal subject matter is made more understandable by a well-organized permanent exhibit on the history and development of holography. Another permanent display is the contemporary portrait gallery. Never have you felt closer to celebrities such as Arthur Ashe, Bella Abzug, Andy Warhol, and Big Bird —all holograms.

Exhibits in the main gallery change every three months, and films on holography are shown continuously during gallery hours. For those who must take a bit of illusion home with them, the museum gift shop has a full line of holographic pendants and stereograms. Or go all out, order a custom-made holographic movie. As a way to capture a space in time, holography is light-years ahead of the camera.

Hours: W-Su: 12-6, Th: 12-9 (except June through August: Th: 12-6). Closed Thanksgiving, Christmas Eve, and New Year's Eve. Admission fee charged.

Free lectures given on Thursday evenings from September to May. Tours by appointment. Research facilities available by appointment for a fee.

Access: Subway: #1, 6, A, AA, CC, E, N, RR to Canal Street. Bus: M1, 6. Car: Parking lots nearby.

135

The Museum of Modern Art

11 West 53rd Street, New York, N.Y. 10019   (212) 956-6100

From Josef Albers to Andrew Wyeth, the Museum of Modern Art's list of works on display reads as a Who's Who of great artists. On one wall is Wyeth's *Christina's World*, with its unanswerable question of whether the woman in the field is straining toward or recoiling from the house on the hill. Across from this realism, the pop art of Roy Lichtenstein's *Drowning Girl*, crying "I don't care! I'd rather sink—than call Brad for help!" Around the corner is Brancusi's sleek sculpture *Bird in Space*. Nearby, to be encountered like a delightful surprise, a colorful Matisse canvas or a fantastic Chagall. And on another wall and around another corner there's more.

What is nice about the setup at MOMA is that the painting and sculpture collection is arranged chronologically, so that a quick survey of modern art from 1880 to 1960 can be had simply by beginning with the Post-Impressionist gallery on the second floor and moving continuously through to the American art circa 1950–1960 gallery on the third floor.

The museum since its founding in 1929 has also been dedicated to expanding the notion of art to include architecture, design, photography, and film. It is not unlikely then to see a toaster or a coffee grinder or a chair on display because of its advanced design.

MOMA was the first museum to acquire and exhibit photographs seriously. The Edward Steichen Galleries on the second floor contain 136 of that medium's masterpieces. Films, shown at least twice daily, are chosen from the scope of international and American, early and recent, independent and commercial work.

A bronze torso by Aristide Maillol was the first work acquired in 1929, when the museum's space was a total of six rooms for galleries, offices, and library. In 1980 the giant Picasso retrospective was mounted, with the entire museum devoted to 923 of his works, over 100 of which are owned by MOMA.

The Modern is now undergoing an enormous expansion program, in which the existing facilities are being completely renovated and a new west wing, including galleries, auditorium, and a 44-story residential condominium, is being built. Presently, over a million people visit the museum annually. After the expansion, that number is expected to increase dramatically.

Photographs taken by Joseph Kugielsky, courtesy of the Museum of Modern Art, New York.

Hours: F-Tu: 11-6, Th: 11-9. Closed Christmas.
Admission fee charged, except Tuesdays by donation.
Baby carriers provided. Lectures in sign language. Picture-taking with tripod by permission for a fee. Research facilities by appointment.
Access: Subway: A, AA, B, C, D to 50th Street; E, F to Fifth Avenue. Bus: M1, 2, 3, 4, 5, 6, 7, 32, 104. Car: Garage parking nearby.

137

Museum of the American Indian, Heye Foundation

Broadway at 155th Street, New York, N.Y. 10032   (212) 283-2420

The bronze doors of the Museum of the American Indian, intricately carved with scenes of Indian life, open onto a cornucopia of fantastic objects from the native peoples of the Americas. From Alaska to Tierra del Fuego, from the Paleo-Indian period to the present, from tomahawks to jade jewelry, from Sitting Bull's war club to Crazy Horse's feathered headdress, three floors of display cases are crammed with examples from the collection of nearly one million artifacts, a collection begun and nurtured by the museum's founder, the late George Gustav Heye.

Loyal to local geography, the museum begins with the Iroquois of New York State. The first display case enlightens you about their lifestyle: charms to guard against drowning (carved in the shape of a canoe), wooden holders used to protect precious feathers between ceremonies, and a tomahawk that doubles as a pipe.

Throughout the first floor, which covers the different regions of the United States, these same kinds of pieces can be seen, often differing in the materials from which they were made. An Iroquian woven vest, for example, becomes a leather vest when made by the Nez Percé Indians, who were great horse breeders.

On the second-floor landing great totems greet you. Here you will find masks made from wood and fur. These are the masks of Eskimos. Worth looking at is case number 110, which contains *The Eagle Dancer*, a fabulous bird costume on a long-haired muscular male manne-

140

quin whose moustache peeks from beneath a painted wood helmet with a huge, hooked beak.

The third floor is a journey south to Mexico, Central and South America, and the Caribbean. Here the showstopper is a case simply labeled *Jivaro Montañas Headhunter*. There is no explanatory text for the contents: gorgeously colored feathers and shells used to decorate arrows and ornamental clothing, plus three shrunken heads and (this is the truth) two shrunken men —doll-like things modestly dressed in loincloths.

But in all fairness, the strange shrunken men are oddities in a collection of thousands of marvelous objects. Here is the chance to learn anew about the Cheyenne, Chippewa, Blackfeet, Sioux, and about other Indians whose names and life-styles are less well known but certainly no less interesting.

Hours: Tu-Sa: 10-5, Su: 1-5. Closed holidays. Admission fee charged.

Lectures for the deaf. Visitors guide in English, Braille, Italian, French, Spanish, and German. Picture-taking without flash or tripod permitted. Research facilities by appointment.

Access: Subway: #1 to 157th Street/Broadway; AA to 155th Street/Amsterdam. Bus: M4, 5. Car: Street parking limited.

MUSEUM OF THE CITY OF NEW YORK

Museum of the City of New York

Fifth Avenue at 103rd Street, New York, N.Y. 10029   (212) 534-1672

The Museum of the City of New York has a personality much like its namesake. This is a spirited, diversified place with an "I Love New York" feel to it—where excited little girls hold hands and screech over display cases of antique dolls, where a mother pushing a baby carriage pauses at an eighteenth-century period room and imagines what it would have been like to live there, where a retrospective of designer Vera Maxwell's clothes sets a group of women reminiscing about the 1940s, where a guard complains to no one in particular that his feet hurt.

And like the city it celebrates, the museum packs a lot into the available space. Four floors in a U-shaped layout display the old and the new, the decorous parlor and the rowdy port, the history of the Stock Exchange and the history of showgirl costumes, without concern for how it all relates. Many of the objects have tales to tell, and in the true New York spirit, their message is never-say-die. Listen to this one:

In the Marine Gallery is a figurehead of Andrew Jackson, carved for the U.S. Frigate *Constitution* in 1834. In the summer of that year an anti-Jacksonite named Captain Samuel Dewey slipped aboard the ship, cut off Jackson's head, and sneaked away with it in a canvas bag. With the literally defaced figurehead draped with a flag, the *Constitution* sailed into New York, a new head was carved, and the repaired Jackson figurehead remained on *"Old Ironsides"* for more than 40 years.

The highlights of the museum are a diorama of New Amsterdam with a 360-degree panorama of the 1660 skyline, Duncan Phyfe furniture, the largest collection of Currier & Ives prints in the world, six period rooms spanning 1690 to 1906, and the most wonderful displays of toys, dolls, and dollhouses.

Museum activities include lectures and concerts, fashion shows and puppet shows, an annual children's Christmas party, and Sunday walking tours of the city's many neighborhoods. Of particular interest is the inspiring multimedia program called "The Big Apple," which tells the story of New York. Save it for the end of your visit; you'll re-enter the real city with renewed vigor and enthusiasm.

Hours: Tu-Sa: 10-5, Su & holidays: 1-5. Closed Thanksgiving, Christmas, and New Year's Day.
Admission free.
Tours in English and Spanish. Picture-taking without flash permitted.
Access: Subway: #6 to 103rd Street. Bus: M1, 2, 3, 4. Car: Garage parking at 102nd Street.

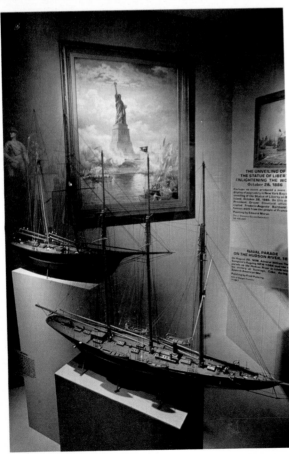

144

National Academy of Design

1083 Fifth Avenue (89th Street), New York, N.Y. 10028   (212) 369-4880

The National Academy of Design is one of New York's venerable institutions, having been formed in 1825. Its 15 founding members included portrait and history painters Rembrandt Peale and Samuel F. B. Morse (who also invented the telegraph), and the list of later members is no less impressive: Thomas Eakins, Winslow Homer, John Singer Sargent, and more recently, James Wyeth, Will Barnet, Raphael Soyer, and Isabel Bishop. In addition to being a membership organization, the Academy is a fine arts school and a museum.

Throughout its history the focus of the National Academy of Design has remained American art. This, along with the work that has influenced American art, is shown at the Academy's Fifth Avenue townhouse gallery.

It is an elegant building, bequeathed to the Academy in 1940 by Archer M. Huntington. A graceful curved stairway with a wrought iron railing takes you from the lobby to the second floor galleries. Additional galleries on the third and fourth floors are reached by an elevator.

The twelve to fourteen exhibitions each year cover a wide range of subjects. You might see a show of architectural drawings (such as the 1981 tongue-in-cheek exhibit of "late entry" drawings for the 1922 Chicago Tribune Tower competition) or still lifes by Italian masters. One exhibit that has been held annually since 1826 is the juried show of contemporary art. Interestingly, the selection process for this annual caused as much controversy 100 years ago as exhibits of its kind do today.

The permanent collection has been developed through a most ingenious tradition: once elected to membership an artist gives one of his works, often a self-portrait. As the Academy has been in existence for over 150 years, the collection of self-portraits and other paintings, prints, and drawings by members is substantial (about 4,200 pieces), and provides a fair representation of trends in American art, such as the Hudson River school and 1930s and 1940s realism.

The only gallery to have a permanent display is the Stone Room on the second floor, where, in a gorgeous hall with three huge arched windows and an inlaid marble floor, there are antique plaster casts of Greek and Roman classic sculpture.

Hours: Tu-Su: 12-5. Closed major holidays.
Admission fee charged.
Picture-taking without flash or tripod permitted.
  Research facilities available by appointment.
Access: Subway: #4, 5, 6 to 86th Street. Bus:
  M1, 2, 3, 4. Car: Street and lot parking
  nearby.

146

The New Muse Community Museum of Brooklyn

1530 Bedford Avenue (Lincoln Place), Brooklyn, N.Y. 11216   (212) 774-2900

In the borough of Brooklyn (which has the largest population of people of African ancestry in the United States) in the section known as Crown Heights (in the early days called Crow's Hill because blacks lived there) is the only museum in Brooklyn devoted to the artistic achievements and cultural heritage of African-Americans. It is the New Muse Community Museum of Brooklyn, located in a large, open, multilevel space previously used by the Brooklyn Children's Museum as a temporary residence.

When New Muse formally opened in 1974 with two exhibitions, *The Black Man and the Sea* and *Two New Muse Artists*, handsome wood cages left by the Children's Museum were filled with doves, finches, and parakeets and a planetarium was operating upstairs. Within this environment there evolved programs and classes in jazz, poetry, dance, art, and photography, and, of course, more exhibits: *The Black Family*, paintings and photos interpreting black family life, with complementing poetry readings and dance performances; *George Smith Meets George Smith*, the work of two African-American artists with the same name. The Thursday night jazz series became a hot ticket.

But in late 1980 New Muse ran into financial difficulties and had to close for seven months. During that time the museum was vandalized and everything not pinned down was stolen. Ironically, about all that was left was a wall-panel exhibit called *The Black Contribution to the Development of Brooklyn*.

But New Muse is getting back on its feet. Their annual Crow's Hill Street Festival has not skipped a year. It is a special day in August for eating African groundnut stew and drinking homemade ginger beer while enjoying the talents of musicians, actors, dancers, singers, and crafts people. Inside the museum the staff is busy collecting heirlooms and memorabilia relating to the settlement of blacks in Brooklyn. They are also creating the *Natural Habitat of New Muse*, a "touch-see" exhibit of live animals and plants for children of all ages.

So stay tuned for the developments, but until then visit the New Muse for the well-documented exhibit on Brooklyn.

Hours: Tu-Sa: 10-6, Su: 12-5.
Admission free.
Access: Subway: #2, 3, 4, 5 to Franklin Avenue.
Car: Take Manhattan Bridge to Flatbush Avenue to Eastern Parkway to Bedford Avenue. Street parking nearby.

147

The New Museum

65 Fifth Avenue (14th Street), New York, N.Y. 10003 (212) 741-8962

What is new about the New Museum? That nothing quite like it exists, of course. The New Museum is a place that fills one of those cracks that artists have always been falling between—the space between ignored and in demand. While alternative spaces are showing work that is being made this instant and traditional museums are collecting, preserving, and exhibiting works of proven historical value, the New Museum is concentrating on art created in the previous ten years.

The New Museum was founded by, and is directed by, Marcia Tucker, who in 1977 left her position as Curator of Painting and Sculpture at the Whitney Museum of American Art amid much public attention and publicity. After curating exhibitions in borrowed spaces for several months, she opened the New Museum coincidentally in the New School for Social Research's Raymond Fogelman Library. The ground-floor gallery is fairly large, but not large enough, so more spacious quarters are being sought.

What this place intends to be is the cutting edge of the most recent developments in art. The museum's obligation is to find art at its sources, and its goal is to be national in scope. For these reasons, Marcia Tucker and the curators travel extensively, and every year or two they showcase art that is being made in other parts of the country. They also have a series, called *New Work/New York*, of provocative work that has not exactly been seen all around town.

Throughout the year in six shows of two months each, the museum presents retrospectives of mature artists whose work has not yet been examined in depth, work of older artists who have not been part of an aesthetic mainstream, thematic shows, and the best work from other alternative art spaces.

In addition to exhibiting art, the New Museum is dedicated to providing documentation and information about the contemporary scene. Its slide library is used in curating the museum's own shows and by other curators, collectors, and artists.

Hours: M-F: 12-6, W: 12-8, Sa: 12-5. Closed major holidays.

Admission free.

Wheelchair access on 13th Street. Occasional lectures and tours. Picture-taking by permission. Slide archives available by appointment.

Access: Subway: #1, 2, 4, 6, AA, B, D, E, LL, RR to 14th Street. Bus: M2, 3, 5, 14. Car: Garage parking nearby.

New York Aquarium

Boardwalk and West 8th Street, Brooklyn, N.Y. 11224 ~~(212) 266-8500~~ 718-265-3474

Some things really are where they should be. Take the New York Aquarium. The New York Zoological Society, the aquarium's keeper, could have carted the toadfish and sand sharks, the platyfish and sea urchins inland, say to Forty-second Street. But no, the New York Aquarium is exactly where it should be—at the edge of the Atlantic Ocean.

A visitor's first sight upon entering is the beluga whales, which look a lot like Pillsbury doughboys. With their little eyes set far back on the sides of their heads, they press their faces against the glass tank and stare back at you. When they're in the mood, they whistle, squeal, and groan at each other, a form of sonar communication. Further along, darkly lit mazes take you through various underwater worlds, with tanks lining the walls. Outside in big pools are dolphins, sea lions, penguins, and a Touch-It Tank for children.

The 90,000-gallon indoor shark tank is a special feature. It isn't every day that you can study so many varieties of our snaggle-toothed friends at such close range, while reading above the tank the kind of information that will frighten you more than *Jaws*. For example, did you know that sharks can detect one pint of human blood within 100 million pints of water?

All kinds of pretty and ugly aquarians can be seen in the various tanks. The longer you look the more you see, since many sea creatures hide themselves quite effectively. It's fun to use the charts posted above the tanks to identify squirrelfish and harlequin tusk fish and lionfish and sailfin tang.

The whales, eels, dolphins, and sea lions put on shows several times a day. While watching Breezy, the adorable sea lion, bounce a ball on her nose, clap her flippers, and catch rings around her neck, you will learn from Breezy's trainer that sea lions can hold their breath underwater for up to 20 minutes and swim about 25 miles per hour.

Hours: Daily: 10-5.

Admission fee charged. Senior citizens free: M-F: 2-5, except holidays.

Research facilities available to professionals in the marine science field.

Access: Subway: D to Brighton Beach, then take M train to West 8th Street/ Coney Island; F to West 8th Street. Cross pedestrian bridge. Car: Take Brooklyn Battery Tunnel to Brooklyn-Queens Expressway west to Belt Parkway to Ocean Parkway south exit. Follow signs to the aquarium. Parking on premises for a fee.

149

The New York Botanical Garden

200th Street and Southern Boulevard, Bronx, N.Y. 10458   (212) 220-8700

On first glance the New York Botanical Garden appears to be an absolutely lovely 250-acre park and woodland where visitors can stroll, jog, and generally enjoy themselves. A second and more intense observation reveals that this park is a carefully planted botanical garden containing such highlights as a hemlock forest, daffodil hill, rhododendron valley, rock and native plant gardens, the Bronx River, lakes, and a waterfall. Still further examination shows that this place is much more than a beautiful park or garden and has been since its founding in 1891.

The primary function of the New York Botanical Garden is to gather and classify plants from all over the world, with an emphasis on those from North and South America. It is a leading research center for plant sciences, and is internationally renowned.

The second function is horticulture and the display of plants, as witnessed throughout the grounds and particularly in the incredible Enid A. Haupt Conservatory.

Function three is education, from classes for adults and children to a program for the training of future botanists and horticulturists to seminars for people in the medical profession on such topics as poisonous and allergenic plants.

The first and third functions have recently been expanded with the addition of three new institutes formed to help solve global problems.

The Institute of Ecology is addressing itself to halting environmental deterioration, Economic Botany is working to develop new food sources from plants, and Urban Horticulture is attempting to identify new plants that resist disease and the effects of pollution in urban settings.

For those who simply want to stroll among the luscious living things, the Enid A. Haupt Conservatory is the place to head for first. Inspired by London's Crystal Palace and built in 1901 to resemble the palm house at the Royal Botanic Gardens in Kew, England, the conservatory is a series of eleven gardens under an acre of glass. The dome, 90 feet high and 100 feet in diameter, rises over a fountain made in Damascus in 1703. Stretching out on either side of this magnificent center are fantastic environments, such as a fern forest viewed from a skywalk overlooking a waterfall, a pool, and a simulated volcanic crater all covered with a vast array of ferns.

Hours: Grounds: Daily: 8-7. Conservatory: Tu-Su: 10-4. Closed Thanksgiving and Christmas.
Admission free.
Picture-taking by permit only.
Access: Train: Take Conrail-Harlem line at Grand Central Station to Botanical Garden/ 200th Street. Car: Take Henry Hudson Parkway to Mosholu Parkway. Turn right onto Southern Boulevard. Parking lot on premises.

153

New York City Fire Department Museum

104 Duane Street (Broadway), New York, N.Y. 10007 (212) 570-4230

For a history lesson from the perspective of fire and water, visit the New York City Fire Department Museum. Here, in a turn-of-the-century firehouse, are three floors overflowing with authentic fire engines and apparatus. You can wander on your own or be taken through by the knowledgeable curator, Lieutenant Clyde W. Williams.

The museum is so wonderfully crammed with objects from the late eighteenth to the early twentieth century that it would be difficult to point out all of the principal pieces. Depending on your particular interests, you may be drawn to the shiny, well-maintained fire trucks, including the hand- and horse-drawn pumpers and early motorized engines that line the first floor. Or the models of firehouses, complete with sliding poles, bunks, and horse stalls. Or pieces of original water mains, made of wood and plugged with more wood, when necessary, as stoppers (hence, the term *fireplug*).

One display case holds a wooden rattle from the Rattle Watch, established in 1648 by Peter Stuyvesant. Watchmen would circulate throughout the city, and when a fire was spotted they shook their rattles to alert the citizens and yelled, "Throw down your buckets." This, of course, was so that a bucket brigade could be formed.

Lieutenant Williams will also tell you that George Washington's image appears on so many pieces of fire equipment because he was a volunteer fireman in Virginia and that we have Benjamin Franklin to thank for introducing fire insurance to America. You'll also learn why the Dalmatian has always been the fire fighter's mascot.

By mid-1982 museum may have merged with the Firefighting Museum of the Home Insurance Company at new location. Call number above for information.

Hours: M-F: 9-4, Sa & Su: 9-2. Closed major holidays.

Admission free.

Lectures and tours in English and Spanish by appointment. Picture-taking without tripod permitted.

Access: Subway: #2, 4, 5, 6 to Brooklyn Bridge; A, CC, E to Chambers Street. Bus: M1, 6, 102 to City Hall. Car: Parking lot on Duane Street.

154

New York City Transit Exhibition

Boerum Place and Schermerhorn Street, Brooklyn, N.Y. 11201   (212) 330-3060

New York's cleanest, most odoriferous subway station can be found at the corner of Boerum Place and Schermerhorn Street. The cars don't travel anywhere, but in an environment unique to life as we know it such small details do not seem crucial. Of course, the station is a museum—the New York City Transit Exhibition. Where else but in a museum would you find a pleasant New York mass transit experience?

You actually enter at the old Court Street station, buy a token, and enter through a turnstile. For once you do not find yourself in a crowded maze that you want to get through as quickly as possible. Instead, the station opens before you, filled with wonderful objects.

There are signals and signs and brakes and lights and the wooden choppers that were used before tokens were invented and were replaced by the first turnstile, introduced in 1922 by General Electric. These artifacts are in no apparent order, which makes a historic tour somewhat difficult. However, they are right there for you to touch and play with, and that is a lot of fun.

The museum auditorium contains the façade of an RR train, and inside its seats are the old rattan variety. Models of the track layout and of trains, past, present, and future, are scattered around, including a state-of-the-art car and station that deserves the wishful-thinking prize.

But the models pale next to what is downstairs—two tracks filled with a variety of old cars. There are the cars used from 1915 to 1965, with their rattan seats and overhead fans. Those who rode such cars to Coney Island will remember them as the vehicle that got them to the beach and boardwalk and roller coaster. Farther along is the first of the IND 8th Avenue line cars, the 1930 model that was Bill Strayhorn's inspiration for the classic swing number "Take the A Train," popularized by Duke Ellington. In 1948 the first stainless-steel car was introduced, and in 1963, especially for the World's Fair, the model with a two-tone blue color scheme and long European-style windows made its debut.

Hours: Daily: 9:30-4. Closed Thanksgiving, Christmas, and New Year's Day.
Admission fee charged.
Access: Subway #2, 3, 4, 5 to Boro Hall; F, A to Jay Street/Boro Hall; M, RR to Lawrence Street. Car: Take Brooklyn Bridge to Adams Street and continue along Adams into Boerum Place to Schermerhorn Street. Garage parking nearby.

155

The New-York Historical Society

170 Central Park West (77th Street), New York, N.Y. 10024   (212) 873-3400

Considering the fact that the New-York Historical Society has a collection of approximately 30,000 paintings, prints, drawings, sculptures, pieces of old silver, glassware, textiles, utensils, furniture, ship models, military weapons, fire engines, early American toys, and more, it is a decidedly harmonious, well-maintained, and graciously quiet place. In fact, without being stuffy, the society is the kind of museum that feels as if it has always been there. And it almost has. Founded in 1804, it is the oldest museum in the city.

On view are permanent exhibits that document the history of the United States, and particularly New York State. Standouts among the profusion include all but two of the 435 original John James Audubon watercolor series, *Birds of America;* a fine assortment of American landscapes from the Hudson River school; beautiful paperweights that capture flowers and fruits and cameos in glass bubbles; and the overwhelmingly realistic if sentimental popular sculptures of John Rogers, which were a part of the decor of almost every middle-class home in Victorian America.

Three galleries of changing exhibitions bring a diverse and up-to-date angle to the museum. Some fascinating shows in the past have been *Manhattan Observed*, where fourteen photographers recorded their impressions of the city's

evolving architecture between 1972 and 1981; *Collaboration: Artists and Architects,* which presented some visionary yet realizable solutions to architectural problems of the 1980s (for example, a bridge that links the World Trade Center with the Chrysler Building); and *That Belmont Look,* artwork, antiques, vintage photographs, posters, and programs to mark Belmont Race Track's 75th anniversary in 1980.

Central to the New-York Historical Society and as impressive as its collections is the library, which contains over 500,000 titles from 1472 to the present and more than a million original manuscripts. Some of the more fascinating documents include the authorization of the Louisiana Purchase, signed by Napoleon; the correspondence between Alexander Hamilton and Aaron Burr, leading to their duel; diaries of slaves; and the rare first printing of Abraham Lincoln's "With malice toward none" inaugural address. Not only is the library's wealth open to public viewing, but visitors are warmly welcomed.

Hours: Tu-F: 11-5, Sa: 10-5, Su: 1-5. Closed major holidays.
Admission by donation.
Picture-taking without flash permitted.
Access: Subway: AA, CC to 81st Street. Bus: M10, 17. Car: Parking lots nearby.

The New York Public Library

Astor, Lenox and Tilden Foundation Fifth Avenue at 42nd Street, New York, N.Y. 10018 (212) 930-0800

Great performers and great audiences can be found on the steps of the New York Public Library at Forty-second Street. All year long (except perhaps when it's snowing) New Yorkers rest, eat lunch, preach, huckster, and watch the constant parade of passers-by from their perch between the two inscrutable marble lions.

At the top of those stairs is one of the most impressive buildings in the city and one of its most crucial institutions. Built in the Beaux Arts style by John M. Carrere and Thomas Hastings and completed in 1911, the huge structure rightfully has the same degree of majesty as the private mansions built farther up Fifth Avenue.

Entering from Fifth Avenue, you walk first into Astor Hall, one of the four spaces used for temporary exhibits. Here, in beautifully carved wood display cases might be found Tom Thumb's visiting card, a seating plan for breakfast with "Der Führer," invitations to the opening of the Brooklyn Bridge, or almost anything from the library's astounding collection of over 6 million books spanning 88 miles of shelves and 17 million nonbook items.

Nothing, it seems, has been too glorious or trivial to warrant gathering and cataloging—from the above items to a Gutenberg Bible, from Babylonian clay tablets to Thomas Jefferson's handwritten copy of the Declaration of Independence, from Shakespeare's First Folio to

T. S. Eliot's typescript of *The Waste Land* with Ezra Pound's manuscript corrections.

The second-floor balcony is another spot where display cases may be found. From here you also can get a better view of the Astor Hall's barrel-vaulted ceiling and its formal ornamentation of carved-marble garlands and rosettes.

The Print Gallery, a hallway on the third floor, mounts three exhibitions a year, and on the same floor in Room 318 is the Berg Collection of English and American Literature, where very special exhibitions of first and important editions, original manuscripts, and autograph letters can be found.

Throughout the building are works of art that in any museum would be central. Here they tend to be overshadowed by the purpose of the place. But outside the Berg Collection is a corridor called the Stokes Gallery, which has excellent prints of North and South American landscapes, and in the third-floor rotunda are wall and ceiling panels painted under the W.P.A.

Tours of the library are available several times a day and are recommended.

Hours: M-W: 10-9, F & Sa: 10-6. Closed major holidays.
Admission free.
Access: Subway: B, D, F to 42nd Street. Bus: M1, 2, 3, 4, 106. Car: Garage parking nearby.

Nicholas Roerich Museum

319 West 107th Street (Riverside Drive), New York, N.Y. 10025 (212) 864-7752

Hours: Su-F: 2-5. Closed June through August and major holidays.
Admission free.
Tours by advance appointment. Research facilities available by appointment.
Access: Subway: #1, AA, B, CC to 110th Street. Bus: M4, 5, 11, 104. Car: Garage parking nearby.

Behind the placid façade of an Upper West Side townhouse is a museum dedicated to the art and life of a most complex, charismatic, and talented man. Nicholas Roerich was one of those rare people whose energy and interests were boundless and whose vision influenced a wide range of people during his lifetime. It seems quite odd that today neither his paintings nor his philosophy is as well known to the general public as before his death less than forty years ago.

When the door is opened and you enter the Nicholas Roerich Museum, you are confronted with a wild burst of color, for along with a sharply focused representational style, Roerich was foremost a colorist. On the right wall are his costume designs for the ballet *Prince Igor*, all in reds and golds; on the wall facing the entrance is a painting of Kanchenjunga, a stark mountain range in the Himalayas.

Throughout the three floors, paintings of peaked mountaintops appear again and again, along with tributes to the lives of the great spiritual teachers (Christ, Buddha, Mohammed, and so on) and symbolic images of the Eastern religions.

Born in St. Petersburg, Russia, in 1874, Roerich managed in his young adult years to juggle careers as a leading archaeologist, painter, and art school director. He also designed costumes and sets for the theater, opera, and ballet, most notably for Nijinsky's *Rite of Spring* (for which he was co-librettist with Igor Stravinsky). During these years, Roerich began to hone a philosophy that blended mysticism, archaeology, and art to create a premise that art unites humanity.

In 1920 Roerich was invited by the director of the Chicago Art Institute to exhibit in the United States. He stayed here until 1923, leaving behind a school of the arts he had founded and a devoted group who promoted his work.

In 1923 Roerich headed a five-year expedition throughout India, Tibet, Mongolia, Chinese Turkestan, Altai, and other remote places in Central Asia. He finally settled in the western Himalayas, living there until he died in 1947.

He had painted more than 7,000 works, but most important, he had designed a peace pact and banner for the protection of cultural property in the event of war. Roerich was nominated for the Nobel Peace Prize in 1929, and his pact was signed in 1935 by President Roosevelt and representatives of all 21 countries in the Pan American Union.

Old Merchant's House

29 East Fourth Street (Bowery), New York, N.Y. 10003   (212) 777-1089

In the middle of warehouses and parking lots, bordering on the Bowery, sits a moment locked in time. The time is the mid-nineteenth century and the setting is the Old Merchant's House, home of the Tredwell family.

Built in 1832, the Old Merchant's house is the only nineteenth-century house in Manhattan to survive intact with its original furniture and family memorabilia. Indeed, most of the furnishings have never left the house, and they are casually arranged as if a family still lived there. The ornate red and gold silk damask drapes are pulled back, the dining room table is set for the eight Tredwell children and their parents, a gown is casually tossed across a bed. The effect is breathtaking. Any minute you expect old Mr. Tredwell to storm into the parlor and demand to know what you are doing in his home.

Here is how this small miracle came to be: Seabury Tredwell, a prosperous hardware merchant, bought the house in 1835, when fashionable New Yorkers were moving from their downtown Wall Street–area residences to Washington Square, Bond, Lafayette, and East Fourth Streets. Gertrude, the youngest daughter, continued to live there until 1933, keeping the house "as Papa wanted it." After her death at age 93, a cousin, George Chapman, pur-

chased and saved the house by founding a non-profit organization to run it as a museum.

Three of the five floors are open to the public. In the basement is the sitting room where the family generally gathered for informal meals and to read and do homework. It is next to the kitchen, with its brick fireplace, original Dutch oven, and hand pump connected to the cistern.

Originally, the two rooms on the first floor were used as parlors. But after Mr. Tredwell's death in 1865 the back parlor was converted into a formal dining room.

The third floor has a small study and two large bedrooms. There are closets filled with dresses, gloves, parasols, bonnets, shoes, and shawls. A commode is modestly disguised as a table. In the front room, against the backdrop of perfect Greek Revival architecture, is the bed where Gertrude Tredwell was born and died.

Hours: Su only: 1-4. Closed August.

Admission fee charged. Children under twelve free.

Tours in English, Danish, Italian, and Spanish. Picture-taking without flash or tripod.

Access: Subway: #6 to Astor Place; N, RR to 8th Street. Bus: M1, 5, 6, 102. Car: Metered street parking and garage parking nearby.

161

The Pierpont Morgan Library

29 East 36th Street, New York, N.Y. 10016 (212) 685-0008, 685-0610

Photographs courtesy of the Pierpont Morgan Library.

The Pierpont Morgan Library is not the kind of place that mounts blockbuster exhibitions that have crowds lined up around the block. It is, after all, as much a research library as a museum, committed to the scholarly interests of Pierpont Morgan and his son, J. P. But for those who enjoy excellent exhibitions of rare printed matter, the Morgan Library is a must.

The collections, begun by Pierpont Morgan when he was a boy in the 1850s and augmented now through gifts and acquisitions, are the finest of their kind. They are the core of the 12 or so exhibitions each year, covering the following areas: Medieval and Renaissance manuscripts, Old Master drawings, early printed books (produced before 1501) and later printed books, early children's books (the first in 1487), autograph manuscripts and letters and documents, bookbindings, musical manuscripts, and ancient written records.

These are fascinating, often beautiful, items to view, but they do require some scrutiny. For example, it is not easy to whiz through twelve centuries of fine bindings and derive pleasure from the experience.

Yet not all the exhibits are so difficult to absorb. About once a year Medieval illuminated manuscripts are shown, and they are fabulous just to gaze at. Every Christmas the complete manuscript of Dickens's *A Christmas Carol* is brought out, and a Gutenberg Bible is almost always on display.

Early in 1982 the Morgan mounted a tribute to Lewis Carroll, the imaginative originator of *Alice in Wonderland,* which included not only manuscripts, first editions, and letters but the photographs Carroll took of his little girl friends, the puzzles he devised, and "The Looking Glass Letters," which are written backward and can be read only when held up to a mirror. And yes, there actually was an Alice—Alice Liddell.

Most exhibitions are held in the large room to the left of the entrance. Smaller shows can be found in the long hallway called the Cloister, which leads to the East and West Rooms. These rooms and the connecting rotunda are decorated in the richly ornate style one would expect from the Morgans. The West Room was Pierpont Morgan's study and is kept much as he left it. The East Room, with three tiers of rare books, is also used for exhibitions.

Hours: Tu-Sa: 10:30-5, Su: 1-5. Closed Sundays in July, major holidays, and August.

Admission by donation.

Wheelchairs available. Tours in some languages by appointment. Research facilities available to scholars by application.

Access: Subway: #1, 2, 3 to 34th Street; #4, 5 to 42nd Street; #6 to 33rd Street. Bus: M1, 2, 3, 4, 5, 16, 101, 102, 104. Car: Street and garage parking nearby.

Police Academy Museum

235 East 20th Street, New York, N.Y. 10003 (212) 477-9753

Some people collect stamps and some people collect coins. Detective Alfred J. Young collects police antiques, and he has been fortunate enough to find a home for them in New York's Police Academy Museum, of which he is also the curator and historian.

Detective Young's extensive collection of badges, uniforms, handcuffs, night sticks, photographs, sheet music, antique firearms, and more is, he says, the best in the United States. Since the N.Y.P.D. is the oldest and largest police department in the United States, Detective Young's objects surely are in their proper place. There they join memorabilia donated by families of police officers and a selection of contraband weapons passed on by the police property clerk.

Because the Police Academy is where recruits are trained, entering the building is not like wandering into a typical museum. An appointment must be made (easy to get), and once there you check in and take the elevator to the second floor.

The museum itself is a very large, meticulously organized room of display cases. Emphasis is on police history, not on crime and weapons. Nevertheless, there are a number of antique and special firearms, including a tommy gun in a violin case and "virtue" pistols, which women carried to protect their honor.

164   Many of the items are extremely rare, such

as a copper badge used in 1845, when the first organized police department was created. At that time, patrolmen wore brass badges and sergeants wore copper badges. The patrolmen liked to call their superior officers "coppers." Hence, the term *cop.*

Old photographs of stern law enforcers and sheets of music with titles like "Oh Girls, Never Trust a P'liceman" and "McNalley's First Day on the Force" re-create the spirit of the men and women who are New York's Finest.

Hours: M-F: 1-5. Closed major holidays. Closed occasionally during the week. Call before visiting.
Admission free.
Picture-taking by permission.
Access: Subway: #6 to 23rd Street. Bus: M15, 26, 101. Car: Parking nearby.

The Pratt Galleries
Manhattan: (212) 685-3169; Brooklyn: (212) 636-3517

Pratt Institute not only trains artists but also exhibits their work in two different locations—one on the main campus in Brooklyn and the other in the Manhattan branch. The two galleries operate both interdependently and independently, sharing four shows each year and curating four or five others on their own. One or two shows at each space are of student work and the rest are drawn from the art world at large.

The Pratt Institute Gallery on the Brooklyn campus is on the first floor of the big, brick Main Building built in 1887. All of its shows are group, thematic, and mostly contemporary, ranging from a survey of figurative sculpture made in the seventies to the notation systems used by dancers and performance artists to the work of older artists from both urban and rural settings who have had no formal training.

Every other year the gallery invites a dozen or so sculptors to create pieces specifically designed for particular sites on campus. This program is called *Sight Sites*. Also on alternate years two artists are invited to transform the two rooms of the gallery into environments.

Pratt Manhattan Center Gallery, at the corner of Thirtieth Street and Lexington Avenue, is where four of nine annual shows open before traveling to the Brooklyn campus. When not exhibiting these joint shows, Pratt Manhattan Center mounts print exhibits curated by that gallery's director for the two first-floor rooms.

The definition of prints at Pratt Manhattan Center extends beyond graphics (although those certainly are shown) to papermaking and political cartoons and even quilts made of hand-printed fabric. One of the most fascinating exhibitions mounted every other year consists of the winners of a petite competition—miniature prints that must not exceed four square inches.

Pratt Manhattan Center 160 Lexington Ave., N.Y., N.Y. 10016

Hours: M-Sa: 10-6. Closed major holidays and August.

Admission free.

Tours by appointment. Picture-taking by permission. Research facilities available to professionals by appointment.

Access: Subway: #6 to 28th Street. Bus: M1, 2, 3, 4, 15, 101, 102. Car: Street and lot parking nearby.

Pratt Institute 200 Willoughby Ave., Brooklyn, N.Y. 11205

Hours: M-F: 9-5. Closed major holidays and August. Admission free.

Tours by appointment. Picture-taking by permission. Research facilities available by appt.

Access: Subway: GG to Clinton/Washington, then walk to campus. Car: Take Manhattan Bridge, then turn left onto Myrtle Avenue, then right onto Clinton Avenue, then left onto Willoughby Avenue. Street parking nearby.

165

Project Studios One (P.S. 1) The Institute for Art and Urban Resources

46-01 21st Street, Long Island City, N.Y. 11101   (212) 784-2084

It might be said that P.S. 1 is the king of alternative spaces. Certainly it wins hands down for sheer size (an entire nineteenth-century schoolhouse). In the vanguard of the alternative art space movement, it can be considered the king perhaps most of all because of the vision and tenacity of its founder and director, Alanna Heiss, who spotted the then-condemned building, persuaded the city that it could and should be utilized, and then proceeded against all probable odds to do just that under the auspices of her umbrella organization, the Institute for Art and Urban Resources.

Since 1976 P.S. 1 (the P.S. no longer stands for public school but for Project Studios) has been mounting exciting and innovative exhibitions and providing space for artists' experimentations, as well as studios for making their art. Artists apply for studio space for one-year periods and are chosen by a committee. They come not only from the city but from Canada, France, Germany, Australia, the Netherlands, and Spain through an international program P.S. 1 has arranged with the governments of those countries.

The building was hardly sleek when reopened, and even now is pretty raw in spots, but the atmosphere throughout the halls and rooms provokes a combination of childhood memories and the sense that anything is possible. You cannot help but feel the surge of creative energy around you. Going to school at last is a thrill.

All available space is a potential exhibition spot: the parapet of the loggia, a broom closet, a windowsill flooded with sunlight. What you see and hear during a visit is a variety of art forms— photographs, architectural drawings, films, video, poetry, painting, sculpture—or any combination thereof. Art at P.S. 1 is often mix and match.

Formal exhibitions are mounted in the first floor's eight galleries and change about every two months. Special projects take place on the second and third floors, and artists are encouraged to welcome P.S. 1 visitors into their studios during openings. The names of the artists who show range from the very-well-knowns to the never-heard-ofs (though you probably will).

What to expect then is the unexpected in a wide diversity of styles. There is something for everyone at the old public school.

Hours: Th-Su: 1-6 during exhibitions. Closed June through September and major holidays. Admission free.

Lectures and tours in English, German, and Danish by appointment. Picture-taking by permission.

Access: Subway: #7 to Hunter's Point; E, F to 23rd Street/Ely Avenue. Car: Street parking nearby.

The Prospect Park Zoo

Empire Boulevard and Flatbush Avenue, Brooklyn, N.Y. 11215   (212) 965-6587

On twelve of Prospect Park's 526 acres live hippos and bears and wooden horses. The horses, painted all colors of the rainbow, are caged in a lovely but decrepit carousel at the southern end of Flatbush Avenue, just a few hundred feet from their 95 neighbors, the animals of Prospect Park Zoo.

Right next to the carousel is the Children's Farm, a kiddie zoo open only during the summer months. A bit farther down the road are five buildings in a horseshoe shape, with bear dens at either end and a seal pool in the center. It is a modest arrangement for a modest array of beasts, who seem to survive in relative comfort in their concrete and iron cages.

Survival, in fact, is the zoo's claim to fame. It has two record holders: Lucky Stripe, born in 1954, is one of the world's oldest living zebras. Banjo Eyes, a spider monkey born in 1957, holds the longevity record for her breed.

Although there was a menagerie in the park as early as 1907, the zoo as we now find it was built in 1935 by the W.P.A. As with Rockefeller Center and other structures that are the results of Franklin D. Roosevelt's program to create jobs during the Depression, the zoo's architecture and details are quite noble.

The central rotunda is the most interesting of the buildings. A mural circles the dome's lip; its theme is the different ways that elephants have been and are used—as work animals, for ceremonies, in the circus. The rotunda houses three cages, of rhinos, hippos, and elephants.

The floor of the rotunda is inlaid to form a compass. In the center of the compass is a statue of a boy and a dog. The boy is hugging the dog, and in one hand he holds a tin can. A most unusual detail is the small hieroglyph etched into the base of the statue, which shows the dog running with the can attached to his tail and the boy chasing after him so he can remove the can. The statue is the "after" scene.

The bear dens are pleasant natural habitats. They are made of mica and granite imported from Kingston, New York. The other cages are small and sparse and a bit sad, but the grounds are well tended by the city's Parks and Recreation staff and trees shade a few outdoor cages.

Hours: Daily: May through October: 11-5; November through April: 11-4:30. Children's Farm: Daily: April through December: 10-4.
Access: Subway: D, M, QB to Prospect Park. Car: Take Manhattan Bridge to Flatbush Avenue to Empire Boulevard. Street parking nearby.

167

Queens Botanical Garden Society

43-50 Main Street (Dahlia Avenue), Flushing, N.Y. 11355 (212) 886-3800

The Queens Botanical Garden is a community kind of place, a garden almost in the backyard sense of the word. It is not lavishly designed on rolling acres; nor does it serve as a botanical research facility of the highest caliber. Instead, by creating a warm and welcoming atmosphere, it nurtures all kinds of visitors as well as all kinds of plants.

It is a relatively new garden as botanical gardens go, having been dedicated in 1963, and like so many cultural institutions in Queens, it got its start at the 1939 World's Fair as a three-acre display called *Gardens on Parade*. That exhibit was donated to the people of Queens and remained open until Robert Moses, in preparing for the 1964 World's Fair, moved its location to the current 38-acre fair site. Unfortunately the entire World's Fair area had been a dump with the Flushing River running through it. An underground tunnel now channels the river and landfill covers the rusted metal, tires, and oil slicks. But even after 50 years, problems still literally arise. Methane gas occasionally bubbles up through the topsoil, killing trees and plants. And once in a while, when someone is digging a new garden, an old sink will be encountered.

Despite these difficulties, masses of flowers grow, birds chirp, and the sun sets spectacularly between the 1964 fair's twin towers and Unisphere. And above all there is color, luscious color that cannot fail to please.

In April and May thousands of tulips bloom, and the summer display of roses is nothing short of glorious. In the backyard garden there are equally wonderful flowers of a more modest nature—marigolds, cockscomb, and zinnias.

The birds and the bees are not ignored. On the Elder Avenue side of the garden is a bee garden with hives that produce up to 800 pounds of honey each year, and along Crommelin Street are varieties of trees and shrubs that attract birds.

Between the birds and the bees is the Wedding Garden, a charming spot where connubial unions do take place. With its white gazebo, gentle stream and waterfall, willow trees, and, of course, more flowers in a rainbow of colors, the Wedding Garden is a lovely sight.

Hours: Daily: 8-dusk. Office closed weekends.
Admission free.
Push-button speaker information system available for the blind. Wedding ceremonies and receptions by appointment.
Access: Subway and Bus: #7 train to Main Street, then transfer to Q44 to Dahlia Avenue. Car: Take Queens-Midtown Tunnel to Long Island Expressway. Exit on Main Street North, then turn left onto Dahlia Avenue to parking lot. Free parking on premises.

169

The Queens Museum

New York City Building, Flushing Meadows–Corona Park, Flushing, N.Y. 11368   (212) 592-5555, 592-2405

The Queens Museum is a light, bright, and witty place that reminds you that art is a pleasure. In a comfortable amount of space, the museum arranges intelligent and accessible exhibitions.

Physically the spaces, clean and open, more closely resemble a private gallery than one's idea of a typical museum. The museum also resembles a gallery because there is no permanent collection. Instead, 15 exhibitions each year are mounted in the main rooms and 10 in the Community Gallery.

From antique and contemporary hooked rugs to whimsical sculpture that harks back to childhood, from the theme of cows to the theme of the 1939 World's Fair, the shows are colorful and fun.

Actually, the subject of the 1939 World's Fair comes up quite frequently. The museum is housed in Flushing Meadow–Corona Park in the north wing of the New York City Building, a block-shaped structure with bands of gold running around the top. Along with the building, the Queens Museum inherited its only permanent installation and one of the world's most fantastic works—the *Panorama of New York City*, conceived for the 1964 World's Fair by Robert Moses, the parks commissioner at that time. New York's masterbuilder set 100 people to work, and three years later came up with an 18,000-square-foot, detail-perfect architectural model of all five boroughs on a one-inch to 100-foot scale.

Viewed from a circular, glassed-in gallery, the panorama is a monumental wonder, with every building, river, street, bridge, and park represented and periodically updated. Special lighting techniques create sunlight, twilight, and night in such a regular and speedy progression that a year can easily pass while you scan the streets for your favorite haunts. All in all the panorama looks much like the view on a clear day when you are on a plane that is landing at one of the airports. It is no less thrilling a sight than Moses's spectacular panorama.

Hours: Tu-Sa: 10-5, Su: 1-5. Closed major holidays.

Admission by donation. Children under twelve free.

Tours and workshops available by appointment. Facilities and programs for the handicapped. Regular film showings. Picture-taking with tripod by advance appointment. Plaster facsimiles of masterpiece sculpture available to art students for sketching by appointment.

Access: Subway: #7 to Willets Point. Car: Take Triborough Bridge to Grand Central Parkway to Shea Stadium exit and follow signs to Queens Museum. Parking available.

171

The Queens Zoo

Flushing Meadows–Corona Park, Flushing, N.Y. 11368   (212) 699-7239

The Queens Zoo, located on the 1939 and 1964 World's Fair grounds, is like a science fiction movie with the following scenario: Once there was a civilization that built tall towers and menacing, snaggle-toothed pavilions. As the culture declined, some citizens took to scribbling over everything in sight. These markings were called graffiti. A terrible mishap of one kind or another has now wiped out all vestiges of humanity. You, the only survivors, wander among the ruins. Wild animals graze in the fields.

Unfortunately, the Queens Zoo has become much like this, and it really is a pity, because the design of the place is remarkable. Instead of being kept in small cement and iron cages, the animals roam freely in fields.

Generally, the animals are from North America—bison, timber wolves, black bear, waterfowl, and California sea lions—although a few immigrants, such as fallow deer from Asia and capybara from South America, have slipped in. The insect house and the dome where the aviary once was have both been shut since the late 1960s, and the snack bar is often closed. The area farthest from the Children's Zoo has an ominous atmosphere.

The Children's Zoo, built to resemble an early American farm, is much more active and in better condition. With the goats lining up at the fence to be fed and the cows and chickens wan-

dering around the yard, it is rather like Old MacDonald's and quite a bit of fun.

The Queens Zoo, along with the Prospect Park and Central Park Zoos, are run by the city. Arrangements are now being made for the New York Zoological Society to take over these three spots, which are sorely in need of attention. No one agrees what it will mean for the zoos, but it is hoped that the Zoological Society will be wise enough to see the potential of the Queens Zoo.

Hours: Daily: 10-3:45.
Admission free.
Lectures and tours by one-week advance appointment.
Access: Subway: #7 to 111th Street. Car: Take Queens-Midtown Tunnel to Long Island Expressway to 108th Street exit. Turn right onto 108th Street, then turn right onto 48th Avenue. Free parking lot on premises.

The Rotunda, Low Memorial Library

Columbia University, 116th Street and Broadway, New York, N.Y. 10027   (212) 280-2877

Start with the rhinestone knee and shoe buckles worn by Columbia University's first president. Add the telescope George Washington borrowed from the college to spy on the British, and a 1780 miniature of alumnus Alexander Hamilton. Contribute a vial of heavy water and the isotope of hydrogen necessary to the making of the atom bomb. Mix in a letter signed by Sigmund Freud, a late-fifteenth-century book of hours, a 1796 treatise on canal navigation with 26 original drawings by Robert Fulton, and a sprinkling of other objects, and you end up with *Treasures of Columbia*—a typical exhibit in the rotunda of Low Memorial Library, the campus's massive central edifice.

Every four to eight weeks the displays in the cases that circle the library's rotunda are changed. Exhibits are organized by different departments of the university, mostly from their own holdings. This means that the cases might be filled with sparkling samples of quartz mined from the depths of the geology department. Or 50 rare books and manuscripts from the library's collection, including Walt Whitman's first edition, first issue of *Leaves of Grass*; a twelfth-century manuscript by Omar Khayyám called *Treatise on Algebra and Trigonometry*;

and Allen Ginsberg's 1956 typed manuscript (with handwritten corrections) of *Howl*.

Once you enter the main quadrangle of the Columbia University campus, there is no missing Low Library. Just look for the steps where the statue of Alma Mater reigns and then allow your gaze to move up to the structure designed in the form of a Greek cross, supported by fluted Ionic columns, and surmounted by a dome that is the largest ever built of solid masonry in America. That dome tops the rotunda where the exhibitions are displayed.

At the east end of the rotunda is Columbiana Library, a handsome space designed to suggest the main reading room in the British Museum. Attached to it is the King's College Room, where you will find on display such interesting memorabilia as a matriculation book containing Alexander Hamilton's name and a chair owned by Benjamin Franklin.

Hours: M-F: 9-5. Closed major holidays.
Admission free.
Access: Subway: #1 to 116th Street. Bus: M4, 104. Car: Street parking nearby, garage parking on 113th Street and Broadway.

174

Schomburg Center for Research in Black Culture

515 Lenox Avenue (135th Street), New York, N.Y. 10037   (212) 862-4000

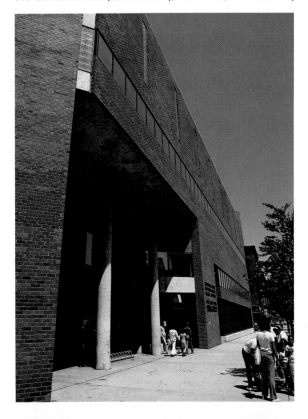

When the Schomburg Center for Research in Black Culture moved in 1980 from its outdated McKim, Mead and White building next door to a new glass and brick residence, the bust of Othello by Pietro Calvi was also moved from one central location to another. The sculpture, so arresting it almost makes you cry, has always been prominently displayed. Inspired in the 1800s by black Shakespearean actor Ira Aldridge, its bronze head and hand peek out from a marble robe; in the hand rests Desdemona's white handkerchief.

The Schomburg houses a history of black peoples who are primarily in the social sciences and the humanities. This is a significant and fascinating collection, started by Arthur A. Schomburg, a Puerto Rican of African descent who as a child was told by a teacher that "the Negro had no history." Sparked by this statement, Schomburg spent his life gathering thousands of books, manuscripts, etchings, portraits, and pamphlets, which became the nucleus in 1926 of the New York Public Library's Negro Division, curated by Schomburg himself from 1932 to his death in 1938.

In the new building the gallery runs along a blind corridor at the right of the entrance. Exhibits, which change about every eight weeks, are always drawn from the library's extensive collection of prints, drawings, photographs, American paintings and sculpture, and African art and weapons. These works are arranged into thematic shows—for example, *Black Portraiture, 1810–1978* and *Black Artists Working Abroad.*

In addition to the gallery, the archives and reference rooms both have display cases that are well worth checking. Here visitors can find exhibits on such themes as rare books and manuscripts (the library holds the original manuscript of Richard Wright's *Native Son*), unique Christmas cards, and a tribute to black women. Scattered here and there are sculptures on permanent display.

Hours: M, Tu & W: 12-8, Th, F & Sa: 10-6. June through Labor Day: M & W: 12-8, Tu, Th & F: 10-6. Closed major holidays.

Admission free.

Picture-taking by permission. No one under eighteen admitted to research facilities unless accompanied by an adult.

Access: Subway: #2, 3 to 135th Street/Lenox Avenue. Bus: M1, 2, 7, 102. Car: Limited street parking nearby.

175

Snug Harbor Cultural Center

914 Richmond Terrace (Snug Harbor Road), Staten Island, N.Y. 10301   (212) 448-2500

With memories of great adventures in Auckland, Rangoon, or the Canary Islands dancing in their heads, retired merchant seamen during the years 1831 to 1976 settled into their last days at a spot overlooking the Kill Van Kull called the Sailors' Snug Harbor. But however disgruntled the old salts might have been about being landbound, they could not complain about the accommodations. Sailors' Snug Harbor was luxurious—a string of buildings said to be the country's finest collection of interconnected Greek Revival structures, plus others in Italianate, Second Empire, and Beaux Arts styles spread over 80 acres.

In its day 1,000 seamen at a time lived there, watching the weather and spinning yarns. But by 1976 most of them had taken their last voyage, and Snug Harbor got culture.

Although the buildings are in need of restoration and renovation, Snug Harbor today is the setting for all kinds of activities: outdoor concerts, art exhibitions, a restaurant, a day-care center, a crafts and fine arts school, a botanical garden, and plans that include a maritime museum and residences for artists. Staten Island Museum and Staten Island Children's Museum will move here by the mid-1980s.

The galleries, named Newhouse and Gallery 3, mount exhibits of contemporary art that change every four to six weeks. In the Newhouse the shows are curated by the gallery director, brought in from traveling exhibitions, or organized by community groups. Gallery 3 is reserved for rental by artists or groups that want to organize their own exhibits.

The lawns are dotted with pieces of sculpture, some on loan from the Museum of Modern Art, some done by New York artists, and some traditional works from the old days. The grounds are cared for by the Staten Island Botanical Gardens, which, in addition to tending the maples and horse chestnuts, have restored a rose garden of over 1,000 bushes and have planted beds of colorful experimental flowers.

Hours: Grounds: Daily: 7-Dusk. Exhibitions: W-Su: 1-5.

Admission free.

Occasional lectures. Tours on Sundays at 2 P.M. and by appointment.

Access: Subway to Ferry: #1 to South Ferry; #4, 5 to Bowling Green; N, RR to Whitehall Street. Bus to Ferry: M1, 6, 15. After Ferry: Bus: #1 to Snug Harbor Road. Car: Turn right onto Richmond Terrace and go two and a half miles to Snug Harbor Road. Limited free parking on premises.

Staten Island Botanical Garden   (212) 273-8200

Hours: Grounds: Daily: 9-8. Closed major holidays.

Admission free.

Free tours of garden on Sundays at 2 P.M. with Snug Harbor tour. Call for dates of classes.

Society of Illustrators Museum of American Illustration

128 East 63rd Street, New York, N.Y. 10021   (212) 838-2560

Lesson number one at the Society of Illustrators is that illustration, removed from the magazine page, poster, record album jacket, or book cover, is art. The paintings of wild turkeys used for Wild Turkey bourbon are, in fact, paintings created especially for the ad by artist Ken Davies.

The images that appear on the covers of *Reader's Digest, TV Guide,* and *Sports Illustrated* magazine were commissioned and painted especially for these purposes. At the Society of Illustrators, these original works of art are exhibited—without the type and other distractions necessary for a successful commercial piece.

The Society does not make a distinction between illustration and fine art except to acknowledge that illustration is work commissioned for commercial purposes. Illustration is Norman Rockwell's all-American scenes; it is an Andy Warhol collage called *Viet Nam Comes Home,* commissioned for *Time* magazine; it is a Gibson girl drawn by Charles Dana Gibson.

Exhibitions, which change approximately fourteen times a year, cover contemporary, historical, and one-person themes. They are drawn from the Society's permanent collection and outside sources. Thematic exhibits have included black-and-white illustration from the turn of the century to the present and how illustrators have treated the subject of romance in magazines such as *McCall's, Redbook, Ladies Home Journal,* and *The Saturday Evening Post.* Four of the exhibits are annual— a juried show, a show of student work, government services themes, and a Christmas exhibit.

The Society, founded in 1901, and the gallery are both located in the carriage house once owned by J. P. Morgan's personal secretary. The first-floor gallery was at one time a squash court. Today, it is a sleek, track-lighted room, joined by a stairway to a second exhibition space below.

Hours: M-F: 10-5. Closed August and major holidays.
Admission free.
Library available by appointment.
Access: Subway: #4, 5, 6, N, RR to Lexington Avenue/59th Street. Bus: M101, 102. Car: Adjacent parking garage.

177

The Solomon R. Guggenheim Museum

1071 Fifth Avenue (89th Street), New York, N.Y. 10028   (212) ~~860-1313~~ 423-3500

Both outside and inside, from the decorative motifs in the sidewalk to the dome that resembles a glass spiderweb, the Guggenheim Museum is a series of curves and arches fashioned from poured concrete. It is the only Frank Lloyd Wright building in Manhattan, and it is almost as startling to encounter today as it was on completion in 1959. It can even be argued that the building upstages the art it houses.

The main exhibition space is viewed from along a cantilevered ramp that winds from the ground to the dome, 92 feet above. It was Mr. Wright's idea that visitors take the elevator to the top and let gravity carry them down the one-quarter mile, pausing along the way at the 74 niches where art is hung. This method of viewing makes some people quite dizzy; others much prefer it to the room-adjoining-room layout of traditional museums.

Art in the Guggenheim begins with the Impressionists and moves forward to the present. The largest group of works by Kandinsky to be found in any American museum and the largest number of sculptures by Brancusi in any New York museum are among the 4,000 works in the museum's collection.

The Guggenheim's exhibitions are ambitious efforts, particularly the retrospectives for which they are well known. The museum's circular design enhances the viewing of an artist's complete oeuvre, since it is possible to gaze across from one section of ramp to another and compare different periods of the artist's work.

The Justin K. Thannauser Collection, located in a room off the main ramp, consists primarily of French Impressionist and Post-Impressionist paintings. Represented are Manet, Renoir, Cézanne, van Gogh, Gauguin, Toulouse-Lautrec, and Degas, among others, plus 34 works by Picasso dating from 1900 to 1960.

The original collection actually was started by

Hours: W-Su & holidays: 11-5, Tu: 11-8.
Admission fee charged, except Tuesdays, 5-8.
Picture-taking without flash or tripod permitted.
  Library available to scholars and museum
  associates by appointment.
Access: Subway: #4, 5, 6 to 86th Street. Bus:
  M1, 2, 3, 4, 41. Car: Park Regis Garage on
  89th Street will give a 15% discount with a
  museum-validated ticket.

179

Study for *Composition II* by Vasily Kandinsky, 1909–10. Photograph by Robert E. Mates. Collection of The Solomon R. Guggenheim Museum, New York

Solomon R. Guggenheim, who hung paintings in his apartment at the Plaza until he had too many. Luckily, full walls did not stop Guggenheim, and he opened his museum in 1939.

A long-distance but most appealing branch of the museum is the Peggy Guggenheim Collection of twentieth-century art, located in a palazzo in Venice. Her collection includes work by Braque, Duchamp, Klee, de Chirico, Giacometti, Dali, de Kooning, Rothko, Gorky, and many others. Needless to say, you cannot get there by subway, but when in Venice a visit is a must.

Songwriters Hall of Fame

One Times Square (42nd Street and Broadway), New York, N.Y. 10036   (212) 221-1252

Al Jolson and Ethel Merman, Victor Herbert and Hal David, Irving Berlin and Dolly Parton, the songwriters and hit makers of the popular song all sit together comfortably with hundreds of their colleagues literally in the middle of Times Square. This is the Songwriters Hall of Fame, on the eighth floor of One Times Square, and it is a thoroughly enjoyable place.

Although the museum is not large, there is something new to see wherever you turn. There's Rudy Vallee's first megaphone and Elvis Presley's monogrammed guitar pick, George Gershwin's custom-built desk and Victor Herbert's standup desk. There are gifts from one songwriter to another—an engraved gold pen given to Hoagy Carmichael by George Gershwin, for instance.

One display has sheet music of every song that has ever won an Oscar. The first, in 1934, was "The Continental," by Herb Magidson and Con Conrad. In all, the archives hold 50,000 sheets of music and 500 original player-piano rolls.

The National Academy of Popular Music, which runs the museum, was begun as a labor of love in the late 1960s by the late Johnny Mercer, songwriter Abe Olman, and publisher Howard Richmond. They were able to open at One Times Square in 1977, when realtor Alex Parker donated the space. Each year new members are elected to the Hall of Fame, and if the list of names is not always familiar, the songs these men and women wrote certainly are.

The Songwriters Hall of Fame is not just a look-see museum. There is "The Do-It-Yourself Room" where visitors can put a roll on the player piano or play tunes on an electric piano, electric guitar, or synthesizers.

Students, senior citizens, and the mentally handicapped are regularly entertained by curator Oscar Brand and staff with piano-guitar-song-and-dance fetes that have everyone in the room clapping and tapping along.

Hours: M-Sa: 11-3. Closed major holidays.
Admission free.
Wheelchair accommodation limited (bathrooms not adjusted). Research facilities by appointment.
Access: Subway: #1, 2, 7, A, E, N, QB, RR to 42nd Street. Bus: M1, 2, 3, 4, 5, 6, 7, 10, 32, 104. Car: Parking lots nearby.

South Street Seaport Museum

203 Front Street (Fulton Street), New York, N.Y. 10038   (212) 766-9020

The streets are paved with cobblestones, the smell of fish makes you wrinkle your nose, and the masts of the tall ships rise above the rooftops. If an historic neighborhood can qualify as a collection, this one certainly does.

This neighborhood—the South Street Seaport —was once the busiest commercial corner of the world. It is the spot most singly responsible for the growth of New York and, in turn, the nation. It is where international trade was hooked into America, where farm and industrial products were channeled from the Midwest after the building of the Erie Canal in 1825, where ships from California docked during the gold strike of 1848. It is where the Fulton Ferry landed on the Manhattan side of its run and where in 1883 the Brooklyn Bridge was built. It is the place that became known as the "Street of Ships."

But by the late 1800s, as sail gave way to steam and increasingly large vessels required the deeper waters of the Hudson, the counting-houses and saloons, the warehouses and hotels deteriorated and were forgotten.

That is until 1967 when the South Street Seaport Museum was created to reclaim the buildings and piers and bring to life the history of the port during the Age of Sail. This ongoing restoration project has grown into the largest in New York City's history.

As a museum, the seaport is a three-part venture: ships, buildings, and exhibition space.

With their masts reaching into the sky as if in challenge to the skyscrapers a few blocks north, the ships are a majestic sight. The grandest of the sailing vessels is the four-masted bark *Peking*, built in 1911 as one of the last commercial sailing ships. Near her are the 1908 *Ambrose* lightship, built in Camden, New Jersey, to mark the entrance to the new Ambrose Channel leading into New York Harbor; the fishing schooner *Lettie G. Howard;* the sloop *Pioneer;* the *Wavertree,* a British full-rigged trade ship; and a city ferryboat named the *Maj. Gen. William H. Hart.*

Exhibitions are currently held at the charming Seaport Gallery at 215 Water Street, which will be expanded to include maritime paintings and displays on the growth of the port and on sail and wind power.

When the restoration is completed, more than four blocks of the neighborhood will be transformed to their active state of years ago.

Hours: Daily: 11-5. Closed Thanksgiving, Christmas, and New Year's Day.
Admission fee charged.
Access: Subway: #2, 3, 4, 5, J, M to Fulton Street; A, AA, CC to Broadway/Nassau. Bus: M15, 23. Car: Parking nearby.

183

Staten Island Children's Museum

15 Beach Street (Bay Street), Staten Island, N.Y. 10304   (212) 273-2060

One year you stepped through a giant pair of eyeglasses to enter the Staten Island Children's Museum. Another year it was the mouth of a 60-foot-long boy, and yet another year there was a bridge to cross. That's because the Children's Museum annually constructs an entirely new, museum-wide participatory environment on themes involving the arts, history, and the sciences.

The glasses were the entrance for a show called *Hocus-Focus,* which was about art and visual perception. Behind the glasses was a maze of displays on shape, line, color, space, and motion, with such showstoppers as an Ames Room, a space in which the floor is slanted and tiles are painted in such a way that when two people stand inside, one appears huge and the other very small.

"Everybody" was the name of the 60-foot-long boy, and it was also the name of an exhibit on the human body. "Everybody" was made of wood, wire, papier-mâché, and cloth—an adorable green-eyed monster of a kid with stations along his body for lessons about skin, the nervous system, the senses, the respiratory system, the digestive system, the skeletal system, and other aspects of the human body.

Once upon an Island presented four centuries of Staten Island life, starring four different ethnic groups who settled in the area—Lenape Indians, Dutch colonists, black oyster fishermen of Sandy Ground, and Italian immigrants. The exhibit, appropriately in the shape of the borough and entered by crossing a bridge, contained over 40 activities set in such scenes as a Lenape village in a quiet forest, a Dutch schoolroom, and a 1920 rapid transit train.

The museum, which opened in 1976 in the corner storefront of an old Brooklyn Union Gas Company office, will be moving to one of the buildings at Snug Harbor in 1983. There it will continue to keep the kind of homey and warm feeling characteristic of the successful hands-on exhibits that continually delight both kids and their parents.

Hours: Tu-F: 3-5, Sa, Su & school holidays: 1-5. Call for hours July and August.

Admission fee charged.

Tours in English and Spanish. Picture-taking by permission.

Access: Subway to Ferry: #1 to South Ferry; #4, 5 to Bowling Green; N, RR to Whitehall Street. Bus to Ferry: M1, 6, 15. After Ferry: Staten Island Rapid Transit Train: To Stapleton. Bus: #2 to Tappen Park. Car: Turn left onto Bay Street, then right onto Water Street, then right onto Beach Street. Metered street parking.

184

Staten Island Historical Society/Richmondtown Restoration

441 Clarke Avenue (Arthurkill Road), Staten Island, N.Y. 10306 (212) 351-1611

Two young women wearing calico dresses sit by the open hearth, calmly stitching while their homemade bread and peach pie send forth enticing aromas from the brick oven. Water is boiling in a caldron so that the women can wash the dishes, and on the table is freshly churned butter for the hot, fresh bread. Over in the next house the harness maker in his baggy breeches and suspenders works on a leather trunk that will withstand tough carriage rides. And just down the street the shelves of Stephens General Store are filled with Borax Soap, Staley's Baking Powder, and gadgets like graters and pitters.

Richmondtown Restoration, administered by the Staten Island Historical Society, is New York City's only historic village. It is 25 buildings (of which 13 are open to the public) on 96 acres that were the Village of Richmondtown. The village, settled by the Dutch, French, and English in the late 1600s, flourished as the center of Staten Island life and as the county seat until 1898, when Staten Island was incorporated into the City of New York. Now structures from the seventeenth, eighteenth, and nineteenth centuries, eleven of them on their original sites, have been restored.

Overlooking Richmondtown from the top of Court Place at Center Street is the white-columned, Greek Revival–style Third County Court House. Across the road is Stephens House and its attached general store. Over on Arthur Kill Road is Voorlezer's House, the oldest known elementary school in the United States, and around the bend are the Basketmaker's House, the print shop, the cemetery, the County Clerk and Surrogate's Office.

Throughout the day young craftspeople dressed in period costumes use the facilities for such activities of Colonial daily life as hand-dyeing yarn, spinning, weaving, baking and cooking, throwing redware pottery, and making furniture.

For visitors who crave "simpler" times, there are courses, demonstrations, and festivities galore—from hoop rolling to barn raising and from paper marbling to period dancing.

Hours: September through June: Sa: 10-5,
  Su: 12-5. Summer: Tu-Sa: 10-5, Su: 12-5.
Admission fee charged.
Access: Subway to Ferry: #1 to South Ferry;
  #4, 5 to Bowling Green; N, RR to Whitehall
  Street. Bus to Ferry: M1, 6, 15. After Ferry:
  Bus: #113 to Richmond Road. Car: Turn left
  onto Bay Street, then right onto Vanderbilt
  Avenue, which becomes Richmond Road. Go
  about 15 minutes and then turn left onto St.
  Patrick's Place. Go two blocks and turn right
  onto Clarke Avenue. Free parking on premises.

Staten Island Museum/Staten Island Institute of Arts and Science

75 Stuyvesant Place (Wall Street), Staten Island, N.Y. 10301   (212) 727-1135.

Hours: Tu-Sa: 10-5, Su: 2-5. Closed major
 holidays.
Admission by donation.
Access: Subway to Ferry: #1 to South Ferry;
 #4, 5 to Bowling Green; N, RR to Whitehall
 Street. Bus to Ferry: M1, 6, 15. After Ferry:
 Walk three blocks. Car: Turn right onto Rich-
 mond Terrace, then left onto Hamilton
 Avenue, then left onto Stuyvesant Place.
 Metered street parking and lot parking
186 nearby.

For a small museum the Staten Island Museum has managed to develop a diverse group of collections. This is the only general museum in the five boroughs to house fine art, decorative arts, natural sciences, and history—all on two floors of a medium-sized building.

As with most enduring institutions, the Staten Island Museum was founded by a group of dedicated citizens who wanted to collect and preserve the culture and natural history of their area and to bring to the island a wide range of fine and decorative arts. That group was formed in 1881, and by 1919 a museum had been built, the same one that houses the collections today.

It is a homey kind of place with a settled and traditional feel, but the museum has outgrown its space and so in the mid-1980s it will move to two of the buildings at Snug Harbor Cultural Center. The Staten Island Museum, along with High Rock Park Conservation Center and the William T. Davis Wildlife Refuge (both within the island's greenbelt), operates under the umbrella of the Staten Island Institute of Arts and Sciences.

In natural sciences, the museum is particularly interested in preserving a record of Staten Island's own history. On the first floor, where this department mounts its exhibits, are displays on geology, flora, and birds. The botanical herbarium contains some specimens older than the institute itself; the highly specialized Philip Dowell violet collection includes types of species and hybrids named by him; and the insect collection, gathered by entomologist William T. Davis, is consulted by specialists from around the world.

On the second floor the permanent collections of fine and decorative arts—5,000 pieces representing the ancient and modern, Eastern and Western—illustrate the history of art in outline form. The museum is proud of the high quality of its silver, prints (spanning almost the entire history of Western printmaking, beginning with fifteenth-century European woodcuts), sixteenth-century Italian paintings, and nineteenth-century American portraits and landscapes of Staten Islanders and the island.

Because of the space limitation, the museum cannot exhibit everything at once, and so it mounts five temporary exhibitions each year built from a facet of the collections and supplemented by loans from other museums, private collections, and galleries.

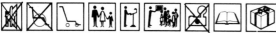

The Staten Island Zoo

614 Broadway (near Forest Avenue), Staten Island, N.Y. 10310   (212) 442-3101

Lions to the left of you, vultures to the right of you. Bats and bears and wolves and badgers, snakes and skunks and tigers and tarantulas—all caged in a gentle, friendly atmosphere at the Staten Island Zoo.

This is not a big zoo; it has only eight acres and animals that have been chosen in proportion to that size. Hence, there are no rhinos or elephants lumbering about, but instead a delightful array of about 850 smaller creatures—from Woofer, a Malayan sun bear, a breed that when mature stands only 3½ to 4½ feet high, to tiny exotic fish that dart around in their aquatic environments.

The Staten Island Zoo's real claim to fame is its collection of reptiles. The rattlesnakes are a particularly fine group, with delegates from all 32 species and subspecies found in the United States. The snakes and lizards slither around or lie still as a stick in the Carl F. Kauffeld Hall of Reptiles, a mysterious tiled room of greens and yellows and blues reflected from the lighting in the glass-fronted houses.

Nearby in the mammal wing is a contender for the Animal Best Able To Make You Shiver award—the small but fearsome vampire bats, which hang together in clusters like bunches of grapes, except when they publicly dine on steer blood daily at 3:00 P.M.

As if to serve as an antidote to these fascinating but creepy creatures there is the great hornbill—a gorgeous, raucous bird with a bright yellow bill and cocky "hat" of the same color. A natural entertainer, the hornbill loves to play with a rubber clothespin and to bellow at a deafening pitch.

Outside in simple, pleasant environments are otters who lie draped over one another in a plush pile of fur, porcupines who trundle about under shaded trees, and pink flamingos who—like a group of yogis—stand balanced on one spindly leg with their heads resting calmly on their backs.

The Staten Island Zoo was the first in the country to have a written commitment to education in its charter. Classes, workshops, and lectures are actively programmed, and there is a children's zoo where the little ones can feed and pet tamed animals. For people who cannot get to the zoo, there is a zoomobile, which carries the animals to the people of Manhattan, New Jersey, and Staten Island.

Hours: Daily: 10-4:45. Closed major holidays.
Admission fee charged, except Wednesdays, by donation.
Lectures and research facilities available by appointment.
Access: Subway to Ferry: #1 to South Ferry; #4, 5 to Bowling Green; N, RR to Whitehall Street. Bus to Ferry: M1, 6, 15. After Ferry: Bus: #107 to Forest Avenue. Car: Turn right onto Richmond Terrace, then left onto Broadway for one mile. Free parking near back entrance.

187

Store Front Museum/Paul Robeson Theatre

162-02 Liberty Avenue (New York Boulevard), Jamaica, N.Y. 11433   (212) 523-5199

Tom Lloyd was one of those who got out of southeast Queens—and one of the very few to voluntarily return. Lloyd, founder and director of the Store Front Museum/Paul Robeson Theatre, was an artist who grew up in that troubled neighborhood. His art took him out of his neighborhood and into Manhattan. But Lloyd became increasingly dissatisfied with the New York art scene and the role (or nonrole) of blacks in it. So he packed his bags and moved back home and slowly began to build a center for his community. That center is located, in Lloyd's own words, "in a poverty area of the first magnitude, encircled by substandard housing, high crime, and marked by an unemployment rate that is the highest in Greater New York."

The name Store Front was chosen because it conveys to the community an idea they can understand. Many churches are in storefronts, so why not a museum of black history and culture. This particular storefront was a Goodyear Tire and Rubber Center with a junkyard lot next door. Today it is a clean, functional space that includes the gallery, a mall, and the 330-seat Paul Robeson Theatre.

The museum was inaugurated in 1971 with an exhibition called *Geographical Scene: West Africa*. Since then it has continued to mount 188 four exhibitions annually, each running for three to four months. Work runs the gamut from paintings and drawings by noted artist Richard Mayhew to art by local schoolchildren to posters in opposition to apartheid to African ceremonial weapons. Graphics by Romare Beardon celebrated the museum's tenth anniversary in 1981 and the dedication of the Rosa Parks Gallery, named for the mother of the Civil Rights Movement.

The Store Front is set up so that everyone who comes must pass through the Rosa Parks Gallery, whether it be for classes in dance, drama, filmmaking, or creative writing or for the frequent community meetings. In this way, by passing through again and again, children learn to appreciate art. And adults, Lloyd says, "who didn't even know what a museum was a few years ago," slowly become regular gallery-goers.

Hours: Tu-F: 9:30-4:30.
Admission free.
Access: Subway: E or F to Parsons Boulevard, then walk twelve short blocks or take any New York Boulevard bus to Liberty Avenue. Car: Take Triborough Bridge to Grand Central Parkway, then bear right onto Van Wyck Expressway. Exit at Liberty Avenue, then turn left onto Liberty Avenue and go ten blocks. Free parking on premises.

The Studio Museum in Harlem

44 West 125th Street (Adam Clayton Powell Boulevard), New York, N.Y. 10027   (212) 864-4500

The Studio Museum in Harlem has come a long way since its founding in 1967. Recently it moved from a former factory loft to a five-story building donated by the New York Bank for Savings, still in the neighborhood where black American culture first experienced a renaissance after World War I.

The museum's sense of purpose is strong. You feel it as soon as you enter. It exhibits and documents black artists and the themes of their art, including the influence of African culture. In many ways that work reflects the community. Often it reflects the streets of Harlem.

Take, for example, the exhibition mounted by the three artists-in-residence for 1980–81. Jorge Rodriguez, David Hammons, and Charles Abramson created an environment in one gallery that was humorous and disturbing, fantastic and real. Using tiles, feathers, Christmas lights, bottles, photographs, old furniture, paint, a television, and other seemingly random objects, they designed "rooms" that evoked poverty yet had qualities of ritual and beauty, even hopefulness.

Next door was a slicker world: black art directors and the range of their work—from products for blacks (Dark and Lovely Hair Color) to products used by everyone but geared in this case for a black market through the use of black models (Con Edison, Miller Beer) to designs that have nothing specifically to do with black culture (a photograph of raw vegetables for the cover of an Italian cookbook, the *Cosmopolitan* centerfold of Burt Reynolds).

Exhibits each year include shows of black masters, emerging artists from a particular region of the world (a different region is chosen every year), the work of the three artists-in-residence, and an exhibition of art produced by children from the museum's Cooperative School Program (which sends professional artists into Harlem public schools). Photography is exhibited in the new James Van DerZee Wing, named for the prominent photographer.

Lectures, seminars, films, concerts, book fairs, and tours of artists' studios and galleries round out the museum's programs, making it a major source of information on black artists and the issues of black art.

Hours: Tu-F: 10-6, Sa & Su: 1-6. Closed major holidays.
Admission by donation.
Access: Subway: #2, 3, A, D to 125th Street. Bus: M7, 11, 100, 101. Car: Street parking nearby.
Note: Name may be changed to Museum of African-American Art.

Taller Galeria Boricua/Puerto Rican Workshop

1 East 104th Street, New York, N.Y. 10029   (212) 831-4333

If El Museo del Barrio is the Museum of the Neighborhood, then the Taller Galeria Boricua (or "Puerto Rican Workshop") definitely fits its role as the same neighborhood's place for working artists.

Located at the southern end of the building that houses El Museo, Taller is yet another facet of the Hispanic artists' community that has become so active in this part of the city.

Since 1970 it has functioned as a collective and an exhibition space primarily for the Puerto Rican community, yet also for the rest of the neighborhood. Mainly Taller provides studio space for eleven artists, but the wide corridor that leads to those studios is also used as a gallery for six to eight shows a year, chosen from outside the collective.

Taller defines itself as a "grassroots organization born from the need to decentralize the dissemination of art and culture from the major art institutions of New York." In other words, the Taller Boricua is a place for the Puerto Rican aesthetic—largely ignored by the artistic mainstream—to be nurtured and exhibited.

This is evident in the work that is shown, whether it be a Brazilian artist's paintings that combine African and Latin American ritual symbols (fish, birds, flowers, stars) or photographs of the South Bronx done in sepia or the *Hidden Treasures* created by senior citizens who live in the neighborhood.

Whether the work is figurative or abstract, the elements that permeate are the events comprising family and community life, from church to street music to love.

Hours: M-F: 10-4. Closed major holidays.
Admission free.
Lectures and tours in English and Spanish by appointment. Picture-taking and research facilities by appointment.
Access: Subway: #6 to 103rd Street. Bus: M1, 2, 3, 4. Car: Street and lot parking nearby.

192

Telephone Pioneer Museum—Carl Whitmore Chapter

88-11 165th Street, Jamaica, N.Y. 11432   (212) 523-3764

In a good-sized room in the black-and-white brick New York Telephone building in Jamaica, Queens, the Telephone Pioneers, a volunteer organization of telephone company employees, run a terrific spot called the Telephone Pioneer Museum. They have been doing this since 1977, particularly for groups of schoolchildren.

The room is chock-full of interesting paraphernalia, which—best of all—you can play with, this being a hands-on museum. A tour begins with one of a number of brief films—perhaps about how to use the phone and its directories or a song fest in sign language for the hearing disabled. The next stop is at an authentic telephone booth where you can eavesdrop on a newly enlisted soldier (a mannequin, of course) having a conversation with his mother.

Display cases along the left wall depict the story of 100 years of telephone history, starting with a replica of Alexander Graham Bell's invention in 1876. There are authentic crank wall phones and the first tall black desk phones and early pay phones, all of which we are accustomed to seeing only in old movies. Traveling into the present, there are today's decorator-style phones, and for the future, a phone that hooks up with a television.

Brief mention is made of other inventors of the phone: Elisha Grey, Thomas Edison, Antonio Meucci (to whom a museum on Staten Island is dedicated), and Abner Dolbear. Still, it is Bell who receives credit for the invention. (It is interesting to learn that both his mother and wife were deaf.)

Scattered on tables throughout the room are phones and switchboards and equipment. You can pick up an old two-digit dial phone and talk to a friend table to table. Or you can put on a hard hat and belt and imagine what it is like to be a telephone repairperson.

Another section shows the things Telephone Pioneers make for the handicapped, such as talking dolls for autistic children and baseball and bowling equipment for blind people.

Hours: By appointment only.

Admission free.

Access: Subway: E, F to 169th Street. Car: Take Queens-Midtown Tunnel to Long Island Expressway to Kissena Boulevard exit. Take service road 2½ miles to 164th Street, then turn right onto 164th Street, then left onto Highland Avenue, then right onto 166th Street. Turn right at 89th Avenue, then right onto 165th Street.

Theodore Roosevelt Birthplace, National Historic Site

28 East 20th Street, New York, N.Y. 10003   (212) 260-1616

Theodore Roosevelt—big-game hunter, Nobel Peace Prize winner, Rough Rider, and twenty-sixth president of the United States—was born on October 27, 1858, in a typical brownstone on a quiet, tree-lined street in the most fashionable residential neighborhood in New York. He lived there for fourteen years, moving, after a year's tour of Europe with the family, to 6 West Fifty-seventh Street. In 1916, three years before T.R.'s death, the home he was born in was completely demolished to make way for a commercial building. Four years after his death, in 1923, a reconstruction accurate as of 1865 was opened to commemorate the only U.S. president to have been born in New York.

The interior was restored with the help of Roosevelt's two sisters and his second wife, Edith, and so accuracy has likely been forfeited a bit to memory and a natural desire to improve upon the past. Only five of the rooms have been reopened, containing about 40 percent of the house's original furnishings. Still, it is as close as we will ever get to seeing Roosevelt's childhood home.

Visitors enter through the servants' basement entrance and move directly into a hall to the right, which is filled with memorabilia—from "Tedie's" christening gown to his 1906 Nobel Peace Prize to wall mountings of the beasts he hunted on three continents.

Upstairs are the parlor and library, opening onto a hall, with a dining room running across the full width of the house at the rear. The third floor has the master bedroom, in which the sickly baby Theodore was born, and next to it is the nursery.

Roosevelt later described the decor as "canonical taste," calling the library a "room . . . of gloomy respectability." He did not care for the heavily carved Victorian furniture with horsehair stuffing there and in the dining room, which he said "scratched the bare legs of the children when they sat on them." But it seems he felt that the highly ornate, many patterned, pale blue silk-damask upholstered parlor was "a room of much splendor."

In the master bedroom is the original rosewood and stainwood-veneered furniture and a portrait of Mrs. Roosevelt, who appears to have been a pleasant woman. In the nursery, pushed against the window, are wooden steps meant to help a child onto the back piazza with its gymnasium. It is here that T.R. vigorously worked out, overcoming severe asthma and other illnesses to embrace the "strenuous life."

Hours: W-Su: 9-5. Closed Thanksgiving, Christmas, and New Year's Day.

Admission fee charged. Senior citizens and children under sixteen free.

Tour pamphlets available in Braille. Picture-taking with tripod by permission.

Access: Subway: #6, N, RR to 23rd Street. Bus: M1, 2, 3, 5, 6, 7. Car: Limited lot parking.

194

Ukrainian Institute of America

2 East 79th Street, New York, N.Y. 10021   (212) 288-8660

The turreted mansion on the corner of Fifth Avenue and Seventy-ninth Street, resembling a French chateau that somehow lost its way out of the Loire Valley, is the rather unlikely headquarters of the Ukrainian Institute of America, a cultural center for people of Ukrainian descent.

The mansion was designed in 1899 either by Stanford White or Charles P. H. Gilbert (there is some dispute about this credit) in the French Renaissance style that displaced the brownstone trend. Although fake chateaus were to remain in vogue for the next 25 years, this is one of the few still standing and it certainly is well preserved. The building was purchased in 1955 by the Ukrainian Institute's founder, William Dzus, a man who made a fortune through the invention of metal fasteners.

Throughout the mansion on the walls of the large rooms and up the wide staircases are paintings by contemporary Ukrainian artists. Most notable among these are the paintings of Alexis Gritchenko, who willed 62 of his works to the institute with the stipulation that these pieces be sent to Kiev if the Ukraine was liberated. Also on permanent display are the figurative sculptures of Boris Kriukow and paintings by Archipenko, the most interesting of which is a sardonic self-portrait showing the art-

ist neatly dressed in a white shirt and tie with his head resting on his hand.

The collection on the fourth floor changes entirely to religious and folk art. Here are brightly embroidered textiles and costumes, including one owned by an eleventh-century princess and a 120-year-old cape brought to the United States by the first Ukrainian immigrant (he had stopped off first in Alaska). There are decorated ceramics and *pysanky* (traditional Easter eggs) and silver found in Berlin after World War II. A small corner room has models that replicate Ukrainian architecture, much of which has been destroyed, such as St. Michael Monastery, built in 1060 and leveled in 1934. Throughout the almost eerily silent mansion is an atmosphere of discontent about the Ukrainian political situation and of emotions held close to the heart.

Hours: Tu-F: 2-6, Sa & Su: by appointment. Closed major holidays.

Admission by donation.

Lectures and tours in English and Ukrainian. Picture-taking by permission.

Access: Subway: #6 to 77th Street. Bus: M1, 2, 3, 4. Car: Street parking difficult; garage parking nearby.

The Ukrainian Museum

203 Second Avenue (12th and 13th Streets), New York, N.Y. 10003   (212) 228-0110

The entrance resembles an apartment building rather than a museum, and the museum itself is on the fourth floor. However, the quiet, modern beige and mustard rooms with cases of festively decorated costumes and jewelry and plates and bowls indicate beyond a doubt that you have entered the Ukrainian Museum.

As much as this is a museum for the general public, it is specifically a place for New York's Slavic community, a large number of whom live in this neighborhood. All explanatory text is bilingual, and the receptionist at the front desk speaks softly to her colleagues in Ukrainian.

The permanent collection of over 2,000 folk artifacts covers the major crafts: woven and embroidered textiles (including costumes), *kilims* (flat woven rugs), woodwork, metalwork, ceramics, and *pysanky* (Easter eggs). For the most part, the objects date from the nineteenth and early twentieth centuries and are aimed at showing the regional diversity in Ukrainian folk art.

The museum's three rooms are not large enough to display the entire collection, so two rooms are used for permanent displays of each type of craft, with objects periodically rotated. In the third room three thematic exhibitions are mounted each year.

With over 1,500 items, the textile collection is

the strongest, and examples from it are the first display you see upon entering. Throughout the museum—on the plates, candelabras, necklaces, and cloths—you note most of all the sophisticated geometric and figurative patterns and the festive array of colors.

Temporary exhibitions (each of which is accompanied by an informative audiovisual presentation) range from *rushnyky*, the cloths used for such occasions as weddings, funerals, Christmas, and Easter, to *samizdat*, the uncensored writings of the Ukraine and Soviet Union.

One of the most popular exhibits each year is the *pysanky* on display from March to June. These Easter eggs are brightly decorated with geometric designs and figures on a black background, their solid appearance belying the fact that such detail has been painted on eggshell.

Those who are interested can learn the art of *pysanky* through a workshop given each year.

Hours: W-F: 1-5. Closed Thanksgiving, New Year's Day, and January 7.
Admission fee charged.
Lectures and tours in English and Ukrainian by two-week advance appointment.
Access: Subway: #4, 5, 6, N, RR to Union Square/14th Street; LL to First Avenue. Bus: M15. Car: Metered street parking and lot parking nearby.

196

The Urban Center

457 Madison Avenue (50th and 51st Streets), New York, N.Y. 10022   (212) 935-3960

What more appropriate headquarters for an organization that is concerned with making cities livable than the Villard Houses, that magnificent complex of mansions so elegantly restored as part of the Helmsley Palace Hotel. Here in the north wing is the Urban Center, New York's first cultural institution to focus solely on the arts of the built city—its architecture, urban planning and design, public art, historic preservation, and landscape architecture.

The Urban Center was established in 1980 and is administered by the Municipal Art Society, a venerable organization founded in 1892. The Municipal Art Society concerns itself with improving the city's physical health (it was instrumental in the formation of the Art, Planning, and Landmarks Commissions and has jumped into the middle of fracases to save such sites as Grand Central Terminal and Radio City Music Hall). The Urban Center acts as the public information source for reports on the improvement or decline of that health.

Sharing the pulse-taking duties are four other groups: the New York Chapter/American Institute of Architects, the Architectural League of New York, the Parks Council, and the New York Chapter of the American Society of Landscape Architects. Together they mount interesting and informative exhibitions that provide some answers to provocative urban questions.

Some of the issues explored are new and old trends (for example, the history of public housing from tenements to high rises), transportation (contemporary designs for public vehicles), parks and architecture and issues such as the impact that budget cuts will have on historical preservation. The exhibits, which change about every three or four weeks, not coincidentally are often timed to fall when certain decisions are being made elsewhere. A terrific bookstore, courses, lectures and seminars, walking tours, and an information exchange (from cleaning brownstones to raising funds for public art) round out the center's programs.

The extraordinary Villard Houses themselves, long considered white elephants, came within a breath of being demolished. That they were saved is our good fortune, but certainly it was no accident—reminding us that it's nice to have the Municipal Art Society as our watchdog.

Hours: M-Sa: 10-5. Closed major holidays.
Admission free.
Wheelchair access on 51st Street. Picture-taking by permission.
Access: Subway: #6 to 51st Street. Bus: M1, 2, 3, 4, 5, 27, 32. Car: Garage parking nearby.

Van Cortlandt Mansion

Van Cortlandt Park, Broadway near 242nd Street, New York, N.Y. 10471 (212) 543-3344

Set far back from car fumes and horns on a three-acre plot (an unusually generous allotment for a historic house in New York) and surrounded by the athletic fields of Van Cortlandt Park sits the elegant Georgian manor house built in 1748 by Frederick Van Cortlandt. The mansion's isolated setting is an appropriate reminder that in their day the home's owners—thanks to slaves and servants who raised flax and livestock, planted crops and acted as laborers—were independent of the outside world.

The Van Cortlandts were indeed a wealthy and influential family, and as such they were hosts to important political figures and party to some of America's historic events. In 1781 alone, their house guests included George Washington, Rochambeau, British Rear Admiral Robert Digby, and the Duke of Clarence, who later became King William IV of England.

Also in that year in order to deceive the British, Washington kept campfires burning all around the house while he withdrew his troops across the Hudson. To the north of the mansion is Vault Hill, the family burial grounds where New York City's records were hidden during the Revolutionary War. The trunk in which the documents were kept can be found in the second-floor hall.

The mansion itself, impeccably maintained, shows both Dutch and English influence.

Outside, above the windows, are satyrlike carved faces called gorbels, which although quite common in Holland were unusual in Colonial architecture. On the second floor of the house are two contrasting bedrooms—one with a Dutch cupboard bed and the other with a canopy bed. Also on that floor is the bedroom where it is sworn that Washington actually slept. The Father of Our Country visited the Van Cortlandts at two pivotal periods of the Revolution—in 1781 to discuss strategy with Rochambeau and in 1783 to start his triumphal march south to Lower Manhattan.

All of the rooms are beautifully decorated with furnishings that for the most part belonged to the Van Cortlandts. The kitchen is a particularly well-outfitted one with such objects as wine bottles initialed VC, pewter plates, and gadgets like a waffle iron, popcorn popper, egg poacher, and pancake maker embossed with a pineapple pattern—the symbol of hospitality.

Hours: Tu-Sa: 10-4:45, Su: 12-4:45. Closed February, Thanksgiving, Christmas, and New Year's Day.
Admission fee charged.
Student classes free by appointment.
Access: Subway: #1 to Van Cortlandt Park. Car: Take FDR Drive to Major Deegan Expressway. Exit at Van Cort. Pk. South sign. Street parking on Broadway, not in park.

199

Wave Hill

675 West 252nd Street (Independence Avenue), Bronx, N.Y. 10471 (212) 549-2055

Imagine standing on the impeccably tended lawns of a magnificent estate overlooking the Hudson River and the Palisades. Those who have previously savored this view include Samuel Clemens (Mark Twain), Theodore Roosevelt, and Arturo Toscanini. All around (but not within sight) are huge, impressive homes; between these grounds and the river is the 96-acre Riverdale Park. The site you are on is called Wave Hill—28 acres of landscaped gardens and greenhouses, on which stand two grand manor houses.

Wave Hill, a glorious horticultural garden and environmental education and cultural center founded in 1965, was built by jurist William Lewis Morris in 1843. After publisher William Henry Appleton purchased the property as a summer home in 1866, he developed the place into a full Victorian estate by adding a greenhouse, a stable, and exotic gardens. Financier George W. Perkins, taking over in 1903, created an 80-acre compound of houses centered around a main house (now Glyndor II) and added more greenhouses, a swimming pool, a tennis court, and a most unusual recreation building—complete with a bowling alley and a gymnasium set underground, and terraces and a colonnade sitting on top.

All of Wave Hill unfortunately does not retain its former glory. The swimming pool, for example, has settled into being an overgrown hole in the earth. But general restoration is taking place, and the gardens, from the 10-acre native Bronx woodland area to the English garden with its colorful array, are absolutely lovely.

One of Wave Hill's most exciting programs is the outdoor sculpture show that runs from May to October. Each year about nine artists are chosen to create sculptures that complement the landscape. This union of art and environment inspires diverse, original pieces that you discover while strolling around the beautiful grounds.

Hours: M-F: 10-4:30, Sa & Su: 10-5:30. Closed Christmas and New Year's Day.

Admission fee charged Saturdays and Sundays. Children under fourteen free.

Access: Subway: #1 to 231st Street, then change to M10 or M100 Bus. Bus: M10, 100. Car: Free parking on premises.

201

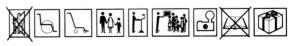

White Columns

325 Spring Street (Greenwich Street), New York, N.Y. 10012 (212) 924-4212

White Columns is an alternative space that has gone through some changes. It started out in 1970 as 112 Greene Street in a large, rough loft at that same address in the heart of what was then unfashionable Soho. According to the current director, Joshua Baer, "112 Greene was a playground for artists who had no place to show." Many of those artists—Richard Serra, Carl André, and Dennis Oppenheim, for example, no longer have such a problem.

Early in 1979 the gallery moved to its current site, an Art Deco building far enough west on Spring Street to practically be in the Hudson River. At this point the name was changed to the 112 Workshop, but this did not really make sense, since the new address was 325 Spring Street. So in 1980 the name was again changed, this time to White Columns.

Programming at White Columns is definitely unconventional. Four artists exhibit simultaneously, each for a one-month period. During that month the artist is free to alter his exhibit, rotating paintings or altogether changing mediums—switching paintings for sculpture or photographs for a video screen. In the evenings there are films, performances, readings, and other events often involving the same artists who are exhibiting. The concept calls for an ever-changing exhibition that, much like a kaleidoscope, has no beginning, middle, or end.

Here are some examples of the kind of work that has been shown in the past and the kind you might expect to see in the future: Marc Blane's green pint-sized wine bottles stuffed with pictures of devastated tenements, an urban rendition of message-in-a-bottle multiplied hundreds of times. Or Jamie Summers's "live" installations—of silk worms that spun and rock salt that grew in triangular configurations and tattoo needles that traced her heartbeat on the gallery's beeswax-covered windows. And now and then art that has been more or less conventionally painted on canvas is neatly framed and hung on the walls.

Hours: Tu-F: 4-11, Sa & Su: 1-11. Closed August and major holidays.
Admission free.
Access: Subway: #1 to Canal Street; AA, CC to Spring Street. Bus: M6, 8, 21, 25. Car: Street parking nearby.

Whitney Museum of American Art

945 Madison Avenue (75th Street), New York, N.Y. 10021   (212) 570-3676

The Whitney Museum is as American as the french fries and ketchup cooked up as soft sculpture by Claes Oldenburg, and as American as the red, white, and blue flags painted by Jasper Johns. It is equally as American as its founder Gertrude Vanderbilt Whitney, who, by the time she opened the museum in 1931, had managed to assemble 600 works, constituting the largest private collection of twentieth-century American art at the time.

Today, having passed its fiftieth anniversary, the Whitney has a permanent collection that hovers around 6,500 objects, including the most significant gathering of works of art by Reginald Marsh and the entire estate of Edward Hopper. From an impressive private collection, the Whitney has grown into one of the most important museums in the world. Its emphasis not only on American art but also on living artists makes it a particularly exciting place.

The building, designed by Marcel Breuer with Hamilton Smith, is a study in scale and light. The exterior of flame-treated gray granite looks like giant steps that have been inverted, leading down into an outdoor well that serves as a sculpture garden. A bridge crossing the well takes you into the lobby.

Inside, mysterious stairways that are indirectly lit lead into spacious galleries where an occasional trapezoidal window frames a glimpse of the city. Even the elevators inspire comments when their huge metal doors open to reveal a space the size of a small room with walls covered in royal blue carpeting.

For the most part the museum is devoted to temporary exhibitions: from small shows on Georgia O'Keeffe, Ad Reinhardt, Alexander Calder, or other artists well represented in the collection to retrospectives and comprehensive exhibits on themes ranging from eighteenth- and nineteenth-century Boston artists to a major exhibition of the art of Edward Hopper to the first museum show to explore the achievements of

Hours: Tu: 11-8, W-Sa: 11-6, Su & holidays: 12-6. Closed Christmas.

Admission fee charged, except Tuesdays, 5-8. Children under twelve with adult, college students with I.D., and persons over sixty-two free.

Tours by appointment. Picture-taking without flash or tripod permitted in unrestricted areas.

Access: Subway: #6 to 77th Street. Bus: M1, 2, 3, 4. Car: Garage parking nearby.

the Disney animators and to honor Snow White, Bambi, and Mickey Mouse.

An exhibition that has become a tradition is the Biennial, a prestigious if controversial invitational of works by living artists. Another important ongoing program at the Whitney is its New American Filmmaker Series, which since 1970 has presented independent films, videotapes, and environmental installations utilizing film and video.

In an atypical gesture for an urban museum, the Whitney has opened a suburban satellite in Fairfield County, Connecticut, at the Champion International Corporation headquarters. The corporate and artistic will again make a match when the new Philip Morris headquarters at Forty-second Street and Park Avenue is completed. By mid-1982 their lobby will house a gallery, and the covered pedestrian mall will have a sculpture court. In the Wall Street area the Whitney Downtown mounts a variety of exhibitions in various locations.

Yeshiva University Museum

2520 Amsterdam Avenue (West 185th Street), New York, N.Y. 10033   (212) 960-5390, 960-5429

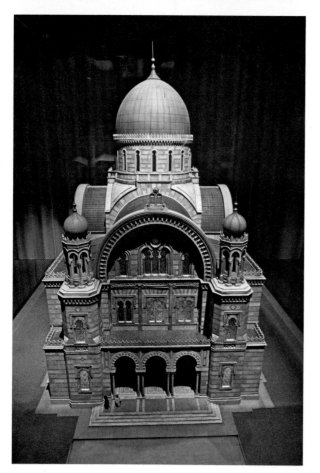

The museum may be modern, but its subject matter is often ancient, more ancient than even Solomon's temple. And when this wealth of material is woven into a fine fabric on a specific Jewish subject, there is an exhibition at the Yeshiva University Museum.

In 1977 it was the Jewish wedding; in 1979 the holiday of Purim; and in 1981 the major exhibition was on daily life in ancient Israel. All the shows link Jewish life and customs—both historical and contemporary—and Biblical law, so that one illuminates the other and the viewer has the pleasure of gaining new knowledge.

The show on daily life in ancient Israel, for example, explained the meaning of a passage from Isaiah: "And they shall beat their swords into ploughshares." Shown were tips of plows with their curled, sharp metal endpieces, easily recognizable as the beaten tips of swords—a natural and practical weapon for farmers who sometimes had to fight.

These year-long exhibitions are well researched and quite fascinating. To derive the most from them tours are available and recommended.

Small exhibits, usually of work by contemporary artists and always on Jewish themes, are changed several times a year.

The museum also owns ten absolutely accurate, built-to-scale models of historic synagogues, including the 1763 Touro Synagogue in Newport, Rhode Island, the oldest Jewish house of worship extant in the United States. Unfortunately, the models are not always on display, but they are beautiful and definitely worth seeing.

Hours: T-Th: 11-5, Su: 12-6. Other days by appointment. Closed June through Labor Day and Jewish holidays.

Admission fee charged.

Wheelchairs limited to the lobby. Tours in English and other languages by appointment. Picture-taking by permission. Research facilities available to students and scholars.

Access: Subway: #1, A to 181st Street. Bus: M3, 101. Car: Garage and street parking nearby.

𝒴IVO Institute for Jewish Research

1048 Fifth Avenue (86th Street), New York, N.Y. 10028   (212) 535-6700

In New York the center for the research and study of East European Jewish culture is the YIVO Institute. It is a rather unique place in a rather unlikely setting: the Louis XIII mansion once owned by Mrs. Cornelius Vanderbilt. Now, in the palatial rooms where once there were fine antiques, a visitor will find a phenomenal and overflowing number of items—300,000 books, 22 million documents, 100,000 photographs and slides, and over 3,000 art and ceremonial objects. These items, many of them absolutely incredible, are the inventory for YIVO's exhibitions in the lobby and second-floor hallway.

YIVO, which is a Yiddish acronym for *Yidisher Visnshaftlekher Institut* or Institute for Jewish Research, was begun in Vilna, Poland, in 1925 to record the folklore, stories, jokes, songs, Yiddish dialects, and other aspects of the 1,000-year-old East European culture. In 1940, when the war and Hitler's regime made it impossible to continue activities in Vilna, the New York branch was opened and has since remained YIVO's headquarters.

Within the wealth of materials found here, startling simply because they have survived, are communal records of town life that date back to the 1700s, one of the largest collections on Yiddish theater, autographed letters from Albert Einstein and Sigmund Freud (both were affiliated with YIVO), and original manuscripts from Sholom Aleichem and I. B. Singer (who is a member).

Certainly the most poignant material is that from the Holocaust: diaries, photographs taken by both Jews and Germans, records of the Judenrat (Nazi-appointed Jewish councils), yellow Stars of David, artwork done by inmates.

And in the corner of the lobby, as if somehow to symbolize the personalities from whose lives such treasures came—and the emotions such material arouses—is a case of expressive little character-study masks for I. J. Singer's play *Yoshe Kalb.*

Hours: M, Tu, Th & F: 9:30-5:30. Closed all
   major American and Jewish holidays.
Admission free.
Lectures, conferences, and cultural programs
   in English and Yiddish. Limited number
   of group tours by advance appt.
Access: Subway: #4, 5, 6 to 86th Street. Bus:
   M1, 2, 3, 4. Car: Street parking limited.

207

Appendix

The following places were not included as main entries for various reasons: some are not yet open but will be in the next year or so, others were or are temporarily closed for renovation or for lack of funding, still others have excellent but limited exhibition schedules, and a few simply didn't fit my criteria for the book but are nevertheless interesting. All are worth a visit, but be sure to call first for updated information.

American Academy and Institute of Arts and Letters
633 West 155th Street, New York, N.Y. 10032/ (212) 368-5900

Three excellent exhibitions featuring American sculpture, painting, architecture, and manuscripts are mounted each year by this prestigious organization.

The American Institute of Graphic Arts
1059 Third Avenue (63rd Street), New York, N.Y. 10021/(212) 752-0813

The three to five yearly exhibitions feature the winners of A.I.G.A. design competitions in such areas as illustration, cover art, and packaging. Other exhibits have included political art and an international array of subway and bus maps.

Astoria Motion Picture and Television Foundation
34–31 35th Street, Astoria, N.Y. 11106/(212) 784-4520

The third floor of the main studio of what was formerly the East Coast division of Paramount Pictures is now a museum of movie memorabilia, including photos, set models, costume designs, and early cameras, TV sets, microphones, and radios.

Brooklyn Public Library
Grand Army Plaza (Eastern Parkway/Flatbush Avenue), Brooklyn, N.Y. 11238/(212) 780-7758

Private sources loan paintings, photographs, and an eclectic range of objects (such as a collec-tion of board games) for exhibitions in the fourth-floor lobby and second-floor gallery.

Cayman Gallery
381 West Broadway, New York, N.Y. 10012/(212) 966-6699

This second-floor Soho gallery with a permanent collection (including carved Puerto Rican *santos*) and changing exhibitions features the work of Latin American artists.

Frances Godwin/Joseph Ternbach Museum at Queens College
Paul Klapper Library, Flushing, N.Y. 11367/(212) 520-7243

Although Queens College has long had an art collection, its new museum has recently begun to mount regular exhibitions on such subjects as the first photographic survey of French monuments and the work of Latin American artists in the U.S. before 1950.

Hamilton Grange National Memorial
Convent Avenue and 141st Street, New York, N.Y. 10031/(212) 283-5154

Currently undergoing restoration, the last home of Alexander Hamilton (who was killed in 1804 in a duel with Aaron Burr) was built in 1801–1802 and occupied by his family until the 1830s. It was named "The Grange" after his family's ancestral seat in Ayrshire, Scotland.

High Rock Park Conservation Center
200 Nevada Avenue, Staten Island, N.Y. 10306/ (212) 987-6233

This 94-acre forested area in the Staten Island greenbelt has a native fern garden, a garden for the blind, a swamp, a pond, and six clearly marked trails (including one for the handicapped). Guided tours are available.

INTAR Latin American Gallery
420 West 42nd Street, New York, N.Y. 10036/ (212) 695-6134

In the pleasant brick-walled lobby of a theater on 42nd Street's Theater Row, INTAR (an acronym for International Arts Relations) presents six annual solo and group exhibitions of the work of Hispanic artists.

Jamaica Arts Center
161-04 Jamaica Avenue (161st Street), Jamaica, N.Y. 11432/(212) 658-7400

This Italian Renaissance–style building, constructed in 1898, is temporarily closed for interior renovation. It mounts exhibitions that change every six to eight weeks on such community-related themes as a history of black photography from 1850 to 1950 and the old Jamaica elevated train.

King Manor Association of Long Island
150-03 Jamaica Avenue (153rd Street), Jamaica, N.Y. 11432/(212) 523-1653

Located in King Park, this one-time home of Rufus King (a statesman and signer of the Constitution) was built between 1730 and 1750. The interior features possessions of the three generations of Kings who lived there.

Museum of the American Piano
211 West 58th Street, New York, N.Y. 10019/ (212) 246-1766

Scheduled to open in April, 1982, this museum features American pianos from the eighteenth century to the present and provides descriptions of the techniques and materials used to make them. The address may change.

New York Hall of Science
Flushing Meadow Park (111th Street & 48th Avenue), Flushing, N.Y. 11352/(212) 699-9400

New York's only museum devoted solely to science and technology is closed for major renovation until 1983. Construction plans include increased exhibition space, a new planetarium, audiovisual studios, and laboratories.

Ratsey and Lapthorn
181 East Schofield Street, City Island, N.Y. 10464/(212) 885-1011

Ratsey and Lapthorn have been sailmakers since 1790. For sailing buffs who are able to identify unlabeled objects, there is an array of presses and fittings.

Sculpture Center
127 East 69th Street, New York, N.Y. 10021/ (212) 879-0430

The Sculpture Center presents solo and group shows of contemporary sculpture in eight or nine exhibits annually. Past shows have ranged from bronze casting to toys made by artists and sculpture for the blind.

Society for the Preservation of Weeksville and Bedford-Stuyvesant History
1698 Bergen Street, Brooklyn, N.Y. 11213/(212) 756-5250

In an alley that was once Hunterfly Road, four homes that were part of the nineteenth-century black community of Weeksville are being restored. One home is currently open and offers displays of artifacts found in the area. It is hoped that the other three homes will be open by 1984.

Staten Island Ferry Museum
St. George Ferry Terminal, Staten Island, N.Y. 10301/(212) 390-5252

In Staten Island's St. George ferry terminal is a small museum containing picture postcards, photographs, models, and ferry parts (such as the steam whistle and the pilot house from the *Mary Murray*)—all relating to the ferry boats that have plied the Hudson since the 1600s.

William T. Davis Wildlife Refuge
Travis Avenue, New Springville, Staten Island, N.Y. 10314/(212) 727-1135

Here are 260 acres of fresh- and salt-water marshland, fresh-water brooks, and upland forests that are home to a wide variety of plants, birds, and animals. Printed trail guides are available and guided tours are offered in the spring and fall.

Index By Boroughs

Categorical Index

Exhibition Spaces

See also Alternative Art Spaces, Art Museums

Zoos and Aquariums

Bronx

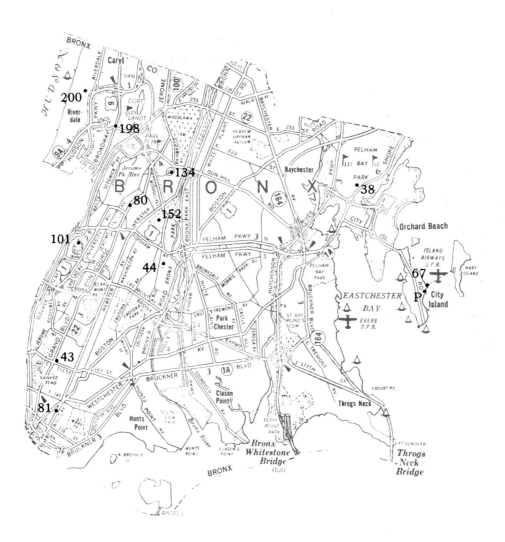

The numbers below correspond to map location and the page in this book where each place is discussed. All letters refer to entries on page 208 or 209.

Brooklyn

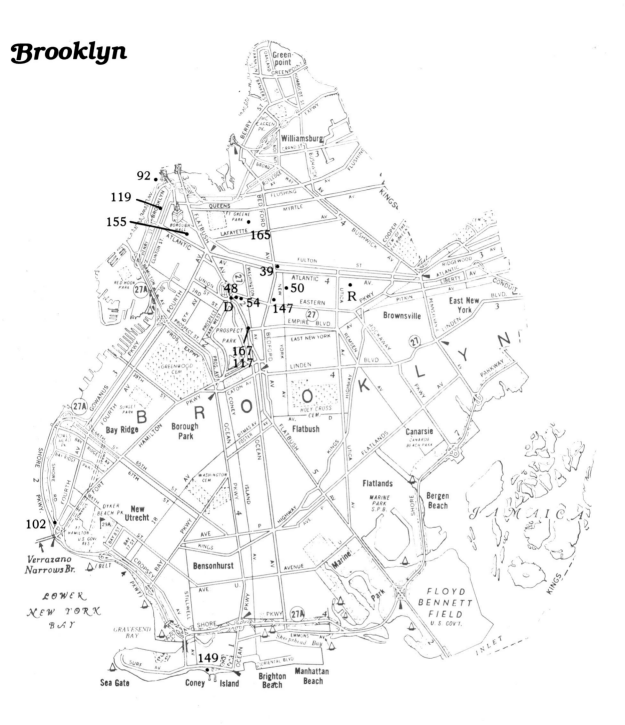

The numbers below correspond to map location and the page in this book where each place is discussed. All letters refer to entries on page 208 or 209.

Manhattan

The numbers below correspond to map location and the page in this book where each place is discussed. All letters refer to entries on page 208 or 209.

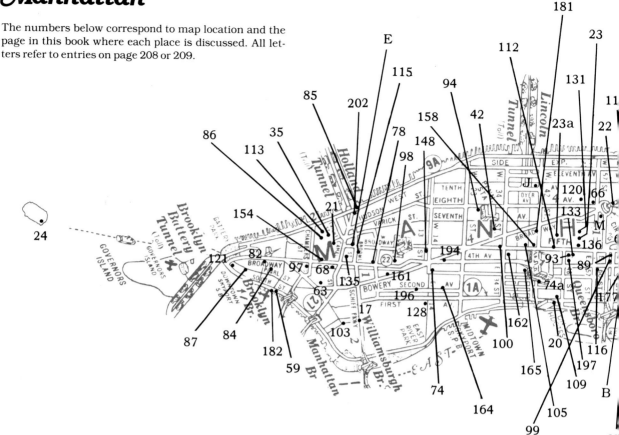

17   ABC No Rio
18   Abigail Adams Smith Museum
20   The African-American Institute
21   Alternative Museum
 A   American Academy and Institute of Arts and Letters
22   American Bible Society
23   American Craft Museum
23a American Craft Museum II
 B   American Institute of Graphic Arts
24   The American Museum of Immigration
26   American Museum of Natural History
32   The American Numismatic Society
33   The American-Scandinavian Foundation
34   Americas Society—Center for Inter-American Relations
35   Artists Space/Committee for the Visual Arts
36   Asia Society Gallery
37   Aunt Len's Doll and Toy Museum
40   Black Fashion Museum
42   The Boxing Hall of Fame
58   Cathedral Museum
 E   Cayman Gallery
59   Center for Building Conservation
60   Central Park Zoo
62   China Institute in America
63   Chinese Museum
66   City Gallery
68   The Clocktower/The Institute for Art and Urban Resources

69   The Cloisters
74   Con Edison Conservation Center
74a Con Edison Energy Museum
76   Cooper-Hewitt, The Smithsonian Institution's National Museum of Design
78   The Drawing Center
79   Dyckman House Museum
82   Federal Hall National Memorial
84   The Firefighting Museum of the Home Insurance Company
85   The Floating Foundation of Photography
86   Franklin Furnace Archive
87   Fraunces Tavern Museum
88   French Cultural Services
89   French Institute/Alliance Francaise
90   The Frick Collection
93   Galeria Venezuela
94   The Galleries at F.I.T./The Shirley Goodman Resource Center
96   Goethe House New York—German Cultural Center
97   The Governor's Room at City Hall
98   Grey Art Gallery and Study Center
99   The Grolier Club
100 Guinness World Records Exhibit Hall
 G   Hamilton Grange National Memorial
31   Hayden Planetarium
103 Henry Street Settlement, Louis Abrons Arts for Living Center
104 The Hispanic Society of America

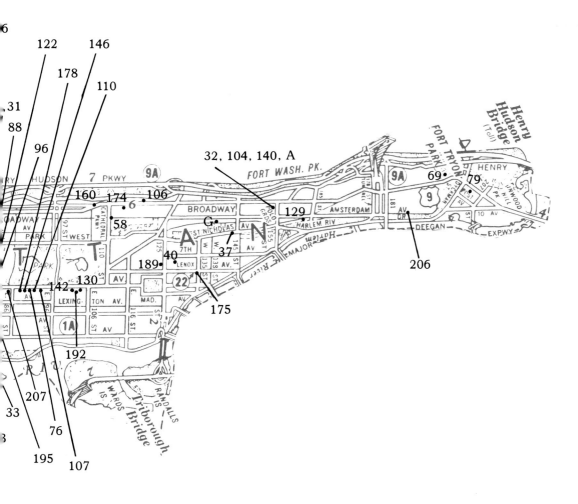

105	The Institute for Architecture and Urban Studies
J	INTAR Latin American Gallery
106	The Interchurch Center
107	International Center of Photography
109	Japan House Gallery
110	The Jewish Museum
112	J.M. Mossman Collection of Locks
113	Just Above Midtown/Downtown
115	The Kitchen
116	Korean Cultural Service Gallery
118	Library & Museum of the Performing Arts/The New York Public Library
120	Manhattan Laboratory Museum
121	Marine Museum of the Seamen's Church Institute of New York and New Jersey
122	The Metropolitan Museum of Art
128	Midtown Y Gallery
129	The Morris-Jumel Mansion
130	El Museo del Barrio
131	Museum of American Folk Art
133	The Museum of Broadcasting
135	Museum of Holography
136	The Museum of Modern Art
140	Museum of the American Indian, Heye Foundation
M	Museum of the American Piano
142	Museum of the City of New York
146	National Academy of Design
148	The New Museum

154	New York City Fire Department Museum
156	The New-York Historical Society
158	The New York Public Library
160	Nicholas Roerich Museum
161	Old Merchant's House
162	The Pierpont Morgan Library
164	Police Academy Museum
165	The Pratt Galleries
174	The Rotunda, Low Memorial Library
175	Schomburg Center For Research in Black Culture
Q	Sculpture Center
177	Society of Illustrators Museum of American Illustration
178	The Solomon R. Guggenheim Museum
181	Songwriters Hall of Fame
182	South Street Seaport Museum
189	The Studio Museum in Harlem
192	Taller Galeria Boricua/Puerto Rican Workshop
194	Theodore Roosevelt Birthplace, National Historic Site
195	Ukrainian Institute of America
196	The Ukrainian Museum
197	The Urban Center
202	White Columns
203	Whitney Museum of American Art
206	Yeshiva University Museum
207	YIVO Institute for Jewish Research

Queens

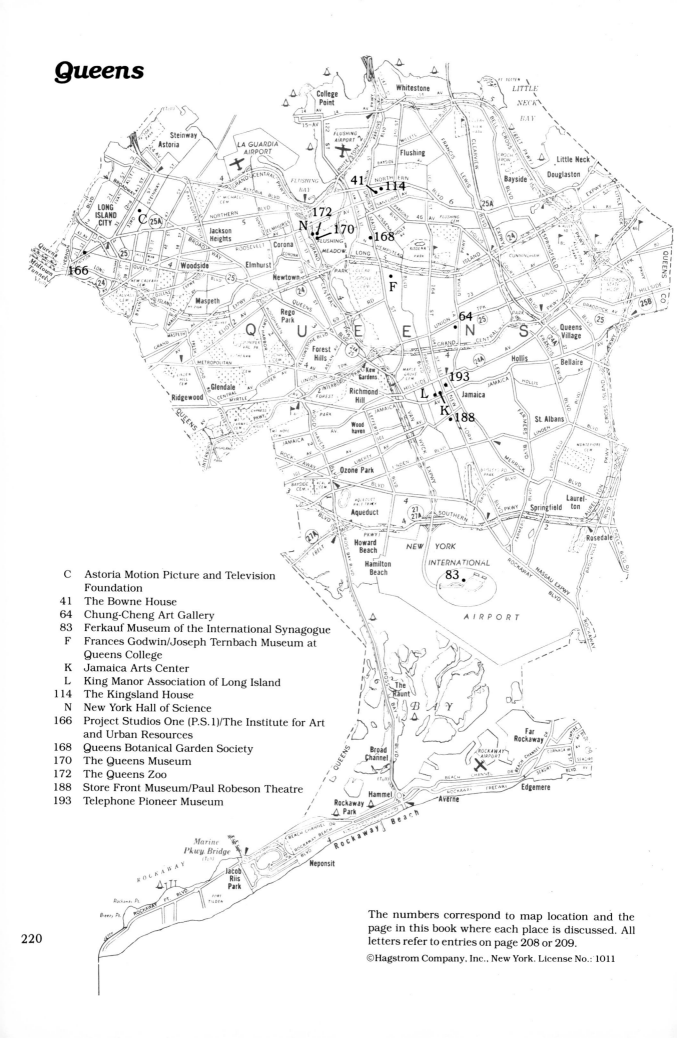

C	Astoria Motion Picture and Television Foundation
41	The Bowne House
64	Chung-Cheng Art Gallery
83	Ferkauf Museum of the International Synagogue
F	Frances Godwin/Joseph Ternbach Museum at Queens College
K	Jamaica Arts Center
L	King Manor Association of Long Island
114	The Kingsland House
N	New York Hall of Science
166	Project Studios One (P.S.1)/The Institute for Art and Urban Resources
168	Queens Botanical Garden Society
170	The Queens Museum
172	The Queens Zoo
188	Store Front Museum/Paul Robeson Theatre
193	Telephone Pioneer Museum

220

The numbers correspond to map location and the page in this book where each place is discussed. All letters refer to entries on page 208 or 209.

Staten Island

The numbers below correspond to map location and the page in this book where each place is discussed. All letters refer to entries on page 208 or 209.

221

Composition in Bookman by TGA Graphics, Inc., New York, New York.
Printing four-color offset on 115 gsm matte-coated paper by
Amilcare Pizzi s.p.a., Arti Grafiche, Milan Italy.
Bound in Italy by Amilcare Pizzi.